# The *Lights* of *Home*

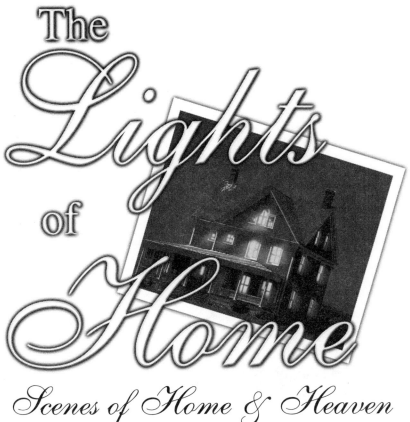

## Scenes of Home & Heaven

# Cindy Sigler Dagnan

COVENANT
PUBLISHING

International Standard Book Number 1-892435-09-8

## DEDICATION

For my heavenly Father who lovingly
thought of and designed the concept of home.
And for my precious daddy
who went Home on July 11, 1998
to turn the lights on for me.
In the twinkling of an eye,
we shall all be Home. . .

# Table of Contents

# Acknowledgments

Thanks to Steve Cable and crew for supporting this project. Thanks to my extended family — all of them — wacky, wise and wonderful, who began the legacy.
Thanks to you mother for choosing our daddy; he was the best. you are so gracious in carrying on without him for now. Because of you, we have always reached for the stars and longed to come home.
Pooh Bear — thanks for being the best of childhood playmates and sisters.
Sigler Sisters and Slinky are a great combination!
Thanks to all who at one time or another have shared our home. Hurry back!
Squeezes and kisses to Eden victoria, Emily Savannah, Elizabeth Grace and Elexa Rose (hard to believe you will join us in 10 short days! Please be on time, if not early!). . . you make homeriotous! Thanks for the wonderfulpriviledge of being your mother. I hope I'll always be welcomed on the fort for snacks. I also pray that you will always feel the pull of the Lights of Home.
Greg you are the undisputed love of my life. You are Rhett to my Scarlett; Captain to my Maria. When I see the lights of home and know that you are there, my heart still beats faster.

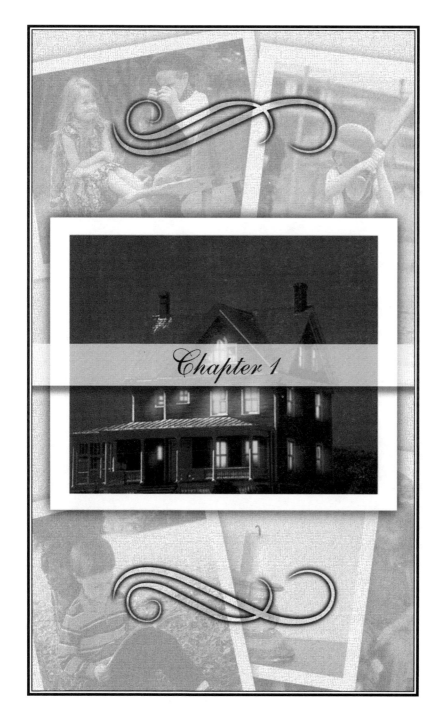

Chapter 1

## Home Plate

*"Home is where one starts from."*
— T.S. Elliot

Funny thing about baseball. You start and end at the same place. Home plate. You run from base to base, shredding the knees of your pants and hurtling headlong into safety. Slides. Signals. Steals. Line drives. Watching coaches. Noisy fans cheering you on (or jeering your errors). Home plate represents victory. And safety.

It's in the spirit of childhood games. "Tag." "No. You don't have me, I'm on home base!" Mother was a base. Porch posts were bases. Oaks and maples were bases. Indeed nothing that stood still was immune from the game. We played on black-topped lots and in brown yards, scorched from the summer sun.

It only took a few of us neighborhood kids and the spirit of the game began brewing. We could hardly contain our excitement. We wanted to start play. Indeed a great beginning is exciting, but it doesn't compare to the finish.

It's the record that counts; the score on the board at the end of the game. Successful runs to home plate. Or stopping the opponent's run to that same plate. Just the other day, I heard my daughter's coach tell the young pitcher: "Now if the ball comes to you, grab it and head for home." Run with me for a chapter, and let's head for home.

## The Lights of Home

If there's anything more satisfying than sliding into home plate with dirt on your face, grass stains on your knees and the roar of the crowd in your ears, I don't know what it'd be. Unless it would be entering the stadium through the pearly gates and having your feet touch golden streets. Watching the saints who've gone before cheer you as you enter heaven and having the One who loved you more than life itself, open His nail-scarred hands and wrap His arms around you, shouting, "Welcome Home! Well done, good and faithful servant!"

But you can't win at baseball unless you stay in the game. Skinned knees, sprained elbows, knotted shoelaces and all. I grew up in St. Louis. Daddy saw to it that I was an ardent Cardinals fan. We ate peanuts from the shell and drank gallons of Coca Cola. We dressed in red shirts, carried binoculars and sang with gusto during the seventh inning stretch. *Take me out to the ballgame* . . . It was contagious, baseball. In fact, my senior year of high school, the Cardinals won the World Series. I got to go to one of the play-off games with Dad and together we later watched on TV the signals of the final play that led the Cards to victory. Thrilling. I learned an important lesson. The only points scored are by those who make it home.

Of course an equally important facet of the game is that you have to follow the set baselines. If you deviate from the marked path, you're out. Period. Next batter up.

Kind of like the little children's chorus: *Oh be careful little feet, where you go. Oh be careful little feet where you go. For the Father up above is looking down in love, so be careful little feet where you go.*

We get in trouble when our feet stray from the path. Just ask Little Red Riding Hood. Or Ahab. Or Lot's wife. . . . or me.

A few Sundays ago, I arrived at church early, because the choir had to practice for our special music that morning. I sang until I had to leave and prepare our classroom for the

14

Sunday School class that I teach. Seems that I left too early, for I didn't hear the choir director's admonition that we exit out the right side only. The left door was apparently stuck and would not open.

After we finished singing, just prior to the sermon, I wondered why all of my fellow choir members were all walking out the same way. *Odd,* I thought to myself. *Oh, well, it's better for me to go out the other side, check on the baby in the nursery real quick and then join Greg* (my husband) *for the rest of the service.*

I exited through the front left door and entered the tiny baptismal preparation area on my way to the back left door. I turned the handle. Nothing happened. I jiggled it. Still nothing. I was perplexed. The room was small and dark and something like panic was beginning to set in.

I had three choices: to go back out the front door and end up next to Sherm, (that's his name, I promise) our minister, who was fervently preaching about the predicament of the lost; to make my way across the baptistery or to stay there for the rest of the service. It was the final choice that I found intolerable.

I paced the four foot space and considered my options . . . I would go for it! I took off my pumps, carried them in my hand and began the perilous journey across the narrow back strip of the baptistery. About halfway across, it became apparent that I was not going to make it. I prepared myself for splashdown and tried hard to think of something intelligent to say when Sherm, as he surely would, parted the curtains to see who was swimming during church.

I teetered, regained my balance and tiptoed backwards, breathing a sigh of relief when I felt the welcome cold of solid, tile flooring.

I began to hope that Sherm might feel led to pray during

the sermon as he'd done sometimes. *Then, I could slip quietly out the front door, ease down the stage steps and take my place in the audience.* Hope began to stir. Sherm was passionately asking the flock to seek out those in trouble. *Hey! Look behind you!* I wanted to shout. After several more minutes, I knew no prayer would be forthcoming. *Surely Greg will wonder where I am and come looking for me?*

*I know! I could hike up my skirt, put on the preacher's waders and quietly walk through the water in the baptistery!* A quick glance confirmed the worst. This was the baptizee's side; the preacher dressed on the other.

Like Pooh, the bear of very little brain, I thought some more. Down on my hands and knees, I felt around in the darkness and located an old bulletin and two highlighter pens. *That's it! I can write a note, push it under the door and then whoever walks by next can open it and let me out!*

I crouched near the bottom of the door and ripped the bulletin into two pieces and shoved one piece in the small ray of light. Uncapping one highlighter I wrote: PLEASE LET ME OUT! and pushed the plea under the door. A few minutes went by and I didn't hear anyone. On the second piece of bulletin I scribbled: HELP ME!!! I poked it outside with my earlier note.

Footsteps approached the door. I knocked softly. The footsteps stopped. "Who's in there?" a voice queried.

"What difference does that make? I obviously can't get out! Please just open the door!"

I heard the knob turning on the other side. I also noticed that on my side, the knob was not moving. *Oh great.*

By that time, my rescuer had identified herself. Sabrina, the teenage daughter of a couple in my class. (Evidently *not* a teenage witch.) "Sabrina," I hissed through the door, "Go get Greg for me, would you?"

Moments passed and I heard more footsteps. They

stopped outside my door. Big pause. Then my husband's voice, confused, whispered, "Cindy?"

"Yes! Let me out!"

I fully expected him to commence rescue efforts, instead, I heard his laugh ring out.

"Hush!" I admonished. "Everyone in church will hear you. Just get me out!"

When his laughter subsided, he informed me that Sabrina had not told him I was locked in, only that I needed him. The two notes in fluorescent pink and neon yellow, lying on the floor in front of the baptistery door had caught him off guard. He promised to look for a screwdriver.

He returned with a kitchen knife. He wiggled and jostled the knob to no avail. The knob had no key hole and no screws. It had been set during the installation of the door.

He came through the other door and looked at me across the expanse of water and shook his head. Sighing, he took off his shoes, and being taller than I am, he leaned across the water and successfully walked the same narrow strip I had previously tried, by grasping the front wall.

When he got to my side, he managed to loosen the knob and remove the locking mechanism, allowing my first glimpse of artificial light. I was thrilled. Incidentally, the incident ended up saving the church a fifty dollar locksmith bill.

But boy did I hear about my off-the-beaten path adventure. I took lots of good-natured ribbing and one couple even made me a survivor's kit. It contained goggles and a straw in case I needed to snorkle, matches to send up smoke signals and a miniature pencil and pad of paper for note-writing.

No doubt about it, where your footprints take you is an important matter. Ultimately, our footprints lead home. Footprints are about influence and legacies, and they can never be ordinary when they have eternal impact. There will be those who come behind us, needing to follow our example on the long journey home. Those who will need to be encouraged by the fact that we stayed in the game.

I love that Steve Green song, "May those who come behind us, find us faithful. . . . May the footprints that we leave, lead them to believe; may the fire of our devotion light their way. . . Oh may all who come behind us find us faithful."

The Hebrew writer gives us an encouraging list of game hall-of-famers in chapter eleven: Abel, Enoch, Noah, Jacob, Joseph, David and many others. They were all players. They all made it home safely.

We have become a nation of spectators, not players; of project starters, not project finishers. Want to change that? Be a project finisher. Stay in the game.

Come on.

I double-dog dare you.

The faithful ones who have completed the game are waving you in; the Umpire is watching your run. It'll be a safe call, I promise. Keep running. Don't give up. Be faithful. Stay in the game. One day soon, you'll cross home plate for the last time. And the first time - forever.

Chapter 2

# A Candle In The Window

*"Home is that place that when you show up there, they have to take you in."*
— Robert Frost

*I* picked a fight with my husband all the way there. "No one walks into a wedding *after* the bride comes in! We may as well stay home!"

Angry words met stony silence. Ten minutes earlier we'd all been in our grubbies vacuuming up eleven pounds of sawdust left by the endless parade of workmen coming in and out while finishing the remodeling of our newly acquired ninety-five year old farm house.

Looking in surprise at the clock, I had marveled that the wedding was about to begin. "Did you know what time it was? How could you not remind me?" I snapped.

"I thought you *knew* since you were taking the time to *vacuum!*" came the pointed rejoinder. No one was ready to go and we lived fifteen minutes away. I sulked. I had wanted radiance. What I got was a dull-eyed, wild-haired sort of wonder. The three children were barely dressed and I looked much worse than Old Mother Hubbard on her finest day.

Now that we were in the van, hurtling toward the ceremony that was to unite two people precious to us, I honed pouting to a fine art.

We screeched into the parking lot, slamming together purses, keys, diaper bags and pacifiers. All five of us had

21

thrown ourselves together, including travel time, in just 16.2 minutes. We slunk (as quietly as anyone lugging an eight, three and one year old sans naps can slink) up the side stair-case to the chapel balcony.

Our three year old, Emily, clutched the railings and peered over the banister, clearly enthralled. Our eight year old sighed at the romance of it all. The baby happily swung her legs over the side of the cushioned pew. *At least some of us are happy.*

The minister had just begun the first prayer after the processional The bride's father had not yet given her away. *Perhaps there's hope,* I thought. The Bride's father lifted her veil and tenderly kissed her. Her hand was placed in that of her husband-to-be.

"Rich Mullins," the minister began, "looking out over the youthful faces of the audience who attended his last concert, said this: 'From now on, you'll get dumber and uglier. This is as good as it gets.' I want you to look at each other and drink this moment in." The audience laughed. The Bride and Groom looked skeptical. They stared at each other with the confident certainty that only the young and naive can feel.

"Why would I begin a ceremony with those words?" he continued. "Because believe it or not, there will come a time in your marriage when you can't get by on good looks and charm. You will be short-tempered with each other. You may experience hard times. You will take each other for granted. Then you'll want to know, what keeps you together during those times? Commitment."

I could feel my husband's eyes boring holes in my back. But I was not yet ready to invite reconciliation.

We listened to the love songs the wedding couple had chosen and watched video chronicling their transformation from infancy to courtship. Then at the end of the ceremony, after vows and rings had been exchanged, they stood together with their parents and lit a single candle.

In the dimly lit chapel, the message was unmistakable. "If this candle represents your marriage, your new life together, you may wonder what possible difference it would make should you ever extinguish that light. It matters. Your oneness is a beacon to the world and an example to all of us who witnessed the promises you made in our presence tonight."

I had not thought of that. I had not thought that our petty arguments could make such a difference in the window of our marriage. But now I did, and I wanted the soot of selfishness and the scorch marks of a critical spirit to be diminished. I wanted the candle to shine through gleaming panes. I offered my husband a tentative smile.

We rode home in a different kind of silence. My husband's big hand enveloped mine. Later that night we worked side by side. Each child was kissed, rocked, read to, put to bed, loved.

We were reminded again of the importance of team work. Of the warmth and comfort of a candle in the window. Of the message our particular candle carried to the world.

*Leave the lights on. The candle's burning.* We are all aware of the homey pleasantness of light.

Light is welcoming. Motel 6 must've modeled their long-running ad campaign after my parents. *We'll leave the light on for you.* The same father who had followed us around during elementary and adolescence flipping off light switches and droning, "What do you think I am? The electric company? Do you think your mother and I are made out of money?" suddenly changed his tune when we entered, The Era of Dating. Now he claimed it wasn't possible to sleep until we were safely home and every light in the house was on. "Come kiss me goodnight when you get in. We'll leave a light on for you!" The porch light and the smaller candles in the front windows never failed to remain lit if any one of us was away. The lights were the first things we saw as we turned onto our street, guiding us home. The lights flickered if we stayed parked in the driveway too long. Those lights saw me through school performances, blind dates, no dates, college vacations and visits back home when I returned with a husband and children of my own.

The candle in the window made such an impression on me that it was the first purchase I made when I moved away from home. It graced the window sill of my college dorm room and the family room window of my first rented home. During our courtship, my future husband, a police detective, knew that if the candle in my window was still on, I would be awake and he could come up to the porch to say, *Goodnight.*

Now in our farm house, we perform a much-anticipated ritual. At dusk, I light candles in every room of our home. The girls follow me around expectantly, inhaling the fragrance of each one and fighting over who'll get to blow them out again at bedtime. The electric candles in all the front windows of our home are also turned on. "Yea, the cozy lights!" claps Emily. Those lights burn until we are ready to retire for the night. They welcome any friends who might happen to drop by and cheer travelers on their way.

We love opening our home to others. We frequently have overnight guests who have dubbed our place, "the bed & breakfast." Sometimes they arrive late at night. "We'll leave the light on for you," comes the assurance.

Such a small gesture. Such a powerful thing.

Ever notice how candle light makes everything more elegant? Beautiful? Ethereal? ["Dark," my husband would point out, as some of you men are doing as you read this.] But seriously, the darker the room, the darker the night, the brighter the candle.

Jesus knew this. "You are the light of the world. A city on a hill cannot be hidden. Neither do people light a lamp and put it under a bowl. Instead they put it on its stand, and it gives light to everyone in the house. In the same way, let your light shine before men, that they may see your good deeds and praise your Father in heaven." {Matthew 5:14-16}

It's hard to hide light. How different might our days seem if we saw all of our actions in terms of light. Our lives as rays of hope that may guide someone home. If the light we reflected was His. If our lives caused others to praise God.

The Psalmist declares God's word a lamp unto his feet {Psalm 119:105} and Samuel acknowledges, "You are my lamp, O Lord." {2 Samuel 22:29}Walking with Him, dwelling in His presence increases our light, keeps our feet on the right path, allows us to practice for life in our forever home.

John writes of heaven: ". . .the glory of God gives it light, and the Lamb is its lamp. . . .there will be no night there." {Revelation 21:23,25}Imagine. A brilliance that eliminates the need for any other light! A Savior whose radiance illuminates all of heaven.

No question that the favorite Sunday school song of my three girls is "This Little Light of Mine." "I'm gonna let it shine," they sing. And then they bellow exuberantly, "HIDE IT UNDER A BUSHEL, NO!!" We talk about what that song means and how their little lives can be blessings of light to others. In fact, the last thing I say to Eden before dropping her off at school each morning is, "Be a blessing today!"

"I want to be a blessing too!" Emily competes. I pat her head and watch as Eden heads for the school door. She looks back over her shoulder and smiles. A light.

Refuse to be part of the gossip. Strike a match. Share a kind word with someone who's discouraged. Kindle the flame. Flash a smile at the man who's just cut you off in traffic. Begin to glow. Let someone go ahead of you in line. In the *express* lane. Increase the wattage. Tell the world in some fashion, each day, about The Light of the World. Burn brightly. Small efforts. Eternal consequences, staking the luminaries on the path toward home.

When she was younger, Eden once looked up at the sky and exulted, "Oh, look! God's home! All his lights are on!" Yes they are. He's leaving them on and watching for our safe return. They'll burn brightly until every one of us has come Home. Never underestimate the power of a candle in the window.

Perhaps in our busy, absorbing world of adult problems and daily struggles we've forgotten to be light. I want to be light, don't you? I want my faith, my attitude and my longing for Home to draw others to the Father. So if we ever chance to meet, I'll try to make sure I've left the light on for you.

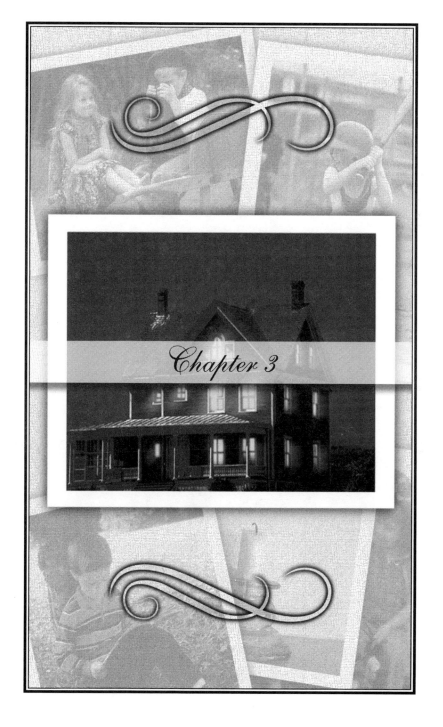

Chapter 3

## Pillow Fights & Oatmeal Cookies

*"Never get so fascinated by the extraordinary that you forget the ordinary."*
— Madalen Nabb

*I* love a good pillow fight. And pillow fights go well with oatmeal cookies. In fact, they're two of my favorite things. They're part of being home along with experiencing siblings. Children. Guests. Life.

Admittedly, our guests are more likely to experience a plate of warm cookies than they are a pillow fight . . . at least on their first visit. After that, the ability to play, to open your heart, your home, your selves—indeed, to become vulnerable is a great gift to give to someone.

Transparent authenticity. At it's best, this is what home is. Home as a refuge. A place where raw emotion and genuine living are welcomed. Where hurts are soothed. Home encourages, shelters and pushes for the best. And sometimes it meets the biggest needs in the most ordinary of ways.

We dare not pass up the ordinary for what appears to be the gourmet. While driving to run errands the other night, I was rushing, hurrying, pushing the limits of speed and endurance. As I rounded a bend in the road I saw it. A lemonade stand perched on the curb of an unkempt lawn. On a precariously balanced tattered card table sat two huge plastic pitchers of some sort of red substance. It looked like

Kool-Aid, but I wouldn't have bet on it. Next to the pitchers, a bag of Styrofoam cups wobbled in the breeze.

As I approached, the eyes of the pig-tailed little girl standing behind it lit up. *A potential customer!* I looked at her tender, innocent, filthy face and suddenly the urgency of the evening didn't seem so urgent.

I slowed down and pulled up to the curb. Exiting from the car, I treated her with my most grown-up manner. Bending down slightly I asked her, "Whatcha got there?"

Her mouth opened revealing that priceless first-grade, gap-toothed smile. "Kool-Aid. Cherry! That's my favorite!" she enthused. And then, more hesitantly, "Are you thirsty?"

"Oh, unbelievably! How much is a glass?"

She pointed to a battered posterboard sign - LEMONADE—10 cents.

"I don't have a dime with me."  Her face fell. "But I do have a quarter, and since I really need to be going, I don't have time to wait for the change, so you'll have to keep it for me. I'm sure it will be delicious."

Dirty hands eagerly poured a glass full of Kool-Aid into a cup whose rim was edged with bits of grass and dirt as though it had blown off the table and been picked up many times. But the proprietess grinned broadly the entire time.

We swapped coin for cup, both of us satisfied with a business transaction well done. She dropped the quarter into a Tupperware box with a hole cut in the top. I thanked her, walked the few steps to my car and drove away.

In the rearview mirror I saw her dance in victory and run toward her house, box held aloft, anxious to share her prize with her parents.

What we might miss by dismissing the ordinary.

And more often than not, home seems ordinary. We fight there. We make up there. We make love to our spouse there.

We rock children. We read stories. We pay bills, wash dishes, fix endless dinners, wash more dishes, fold loads of laundry that multiply faster than fruit flies on a rotten banana.

We mark time there. We turn over the calendar pages to new month after new month after new month. We sweep floors, scrub toilets, wash windows. We dust furniture, dance, talk on the phone and pray on our knees at bedtime.

We've kept all night vigils at the bedside of a sick child. We've entertained guests with backyard bar-b-ques, front porch visits and overnights on thick floor pallets. It's been the first ever destination of brand new babies fresh from the hospital, their mother's womb and the hand of God. We've also returned home from a funeral with one place setting forever missing. One chair empty at family gatherings.

We've laughed. Cried. Been ridiculous and silly. We've dreamed there and even seen some of those dreams come true.

We rake leaves in the fall, shovel snow in the winter, watch the tulips push up every spring and mow the lawn all summer.

None of it *seems* extraordinary. But oh, it is! Scripture says that life is "few of days and full of trouble," but deliberate merriment and careful appreciation lighten the load. {Job 14:1, NKJV}

For some reason our girls have taken a fancy to playing a game they call "poor." They like to go in one of their closets (usually Eden's, because she is the oldest and her younger sisters are in proper awe when she allows them to enter her domain) and drape doll blankets over every conceivable shelf. They take plastic foodstuffs and baby dolls by the wagon load into the closet. And there they hibernate. Reading books by flashlight. Giggling. Singing.

The other night after a rousing session of bill paying on

pay day (why is it that you always need another pay day immediately following this monthly ritual?) the girls circled my chair at the kitchen table like baby vultures.

"You ask her, you're littler," Eden hissed.

"Huh-uh. You're the oldest," Emmy bargained.

They both looked at baby Ellie. "Mama, play?" she chirped.

All three of them joined forces and I was spirited away to the closet to play "poor." I can't think of a single specific thing we did that I could label extraordinary. I'm sure we exchanged whispered confidences, giddy girl secrets and general laughter. What I do know is that I came out twenty minutes later feeling extremely rich.

Maybe it's a good thing to play "poor" every now and then. For as Mary Pipher in her wonderful book, *The Shelter of Each Other,* says, too much of the world can make our children and ourselves "want good things instead of good lives."

I have learned lessons through the notes and messages that the children, their father and I exchange in our tiny individual mailboxes, nailed to the wall outside each bedroom door.

Eden to Emmy: *I'm sorry I told you I wouldn't play with you anymore. I didn't mean it. We'll be sisters forever and ever, I promise!*

Emmy to Eden: [since Emmy's just four, she prints her name, writes a bunch of curlicues and interprets for us] *You can have one of my bestest Barbies. For Keeps! I love you, Emmy*

Another day, Eden brings home candy and stickers from school for her sisters and delivered them to be discovered later with much joy.

Eden to Mommy: *Sometimes I think you're too bossy. Thanks for letting me tell you that though. I love you anyway.*

Mommy to Eden: *Practice your piano and put away your*

*clothes before you go play. Love you, Stinkerbell.*

Eden to Mommy & Daddy: *I'm sorry I've been arguing so much lately. I'm really trying, thanks for loving me. P.S. Don't forget I need book money, lunch money, milk money and treat money for tomorrow. P.P.S. Can Haley play after school?*

Private love notes and funny cartoons left in Greg's and my mailbox to each other, especially if one of us is leaving town.

And from Ellie, random Tinker Toy pieces and tiny books. Invariably, she wants them back later.

There are days we forget, weeks even, to leave anything for each other. Days we forget to play, days we squander our precious time together. Sometimes the children have to remind their harried parents to check their mailbox and make time to play.

Children know the inherent gifts of oatmeal cookies and pillow fights. That's why it is so much fun to start either project with them. A sturdy "fight" results in breathless cries of "Again, daddy!" Giving each child a turn with the electric mixer and trying not to mind too much when much of the dough covers their hair and counters instead of the cookie sheets, we then retreat to the wooden fort with a plate of warm cookies, the fruit of our labors, for after-school snacks.

I am thankful for those times. Children push at the edges of our concrete ideas and boundaries. Our ideas of what should and should not be. They introduce flexibility and spontaneity into the ruts of life. They constantly question. "Why?" "When?" "Where?" "How come?" And they have a way of making home anything but ordinary.

In the car yesterday on our way to pick up Eden from school, I glanced in the rearview mirror. A still sleepy Emmy and Ellie were buckled into their carseats, hair and faces warm and tousled from their naps, staring back at me with sweet smiles. My heart flooded with overwhelming gratitude.

"Oh my little girls! Are you always going to stay my little girls?" I burst out, heedless of whether or not I sounded like a cheesy rewrite of *Little Women*.

Emmy shouted, "I am!"

Not to be outdone, Ellie chimed in, "Me am!"

Then Emmy reconsidered. "But Mommy, if I ever change my mind, I will build my house right next to yours!"

Good enough.

Bodie Thoene in her insightful novel, *In My Father's House*, describes perfectly the unparalleled allure of home. Any home. Jefferson Canfield, a poor black sharecropper and preacher, returning from the battles of World War I, arrives home after a long tedious, tumultuous journey by boat, train and foot. Footsore and heartsick, he arrives at a tiny rough hewn log cabin, the only home he has ever known. His father, mother, brothers and sisters enfold him in a warm circle of love and jubilant excitement. That night, as he lays down on his mattress in front of the fire, covered by a simple homemade quilt, he announces with heartfelt thanks, "This ain't heaven, but it's home, and home's the next best thing to heaven."

I have to agree. Home is God's gracious gift to us while we are caught in this sweet time warp between the now and the not yet. Jane Canfield wrote, "Happy people do not depend on excitement. . . supplied by externals. They enjoy the fundamental, often very simple things of life. They savor the moment, glad to be alive, enjoying their work, their families, the good things around them."

Home is one of those "good things." It is a constant reminder to us that there may be a measure of grace in a pillow fight; mercy in a dirty cup of lemonade; pieces of heaven on a plate of warm oatmeal cookies.

Chapter 4

*Home Movies*
*& Heart*
*Pictures*

*"Every day in a life fills the whole life with expectation and memory."*
— C.S. Lewis

side from the fact that I was on my way to a funeral, I could just tell that it was going to be one of those days. My neighbor and good friend's mother had died and the family had asked me to sing and play the piano at her services.

Enroute, I stopped at my mother's house to drop off the three little girls. I hastily gave my mother instructions and buckled the carseats into her car so they could go to the park. When I emerged from the backseat, my mother stared at my right knee and pointed in horror. Glancing down I saw the problem. A neon green Crayon had melted all over the car's upholstery (did I mention it was ninety-five degrees and I was dressed head-to-toe in black?) and I had stuck my knee smack dab in the middle of the waxy puddle.

My sheer black hose now sported a baseball-sized glob of glowing green, complete with charming chips of still-intact crayon stuck to my knee in a random pattern. It looked a small space alien had imploded on my kneecap.

I looked forlornly at my mother and I could tell she was ready to burst out laughing. But by now it was clear that if I didn't leave *this instant,* I would be late. So I quickly practiced holding my purse nonchalantly in front of the stain by leaning a little to one side.

37

"With any luck that side of me will be to the wall," I quipped.

I arrived at the funeral home with five minutes to spare before the prelude music was to begin. I cased the room. No piano.

I scrounged up one usher, one funeral director and a mortician. "Where," I ventured, "is the piano I was told would be here?"

The tallest Suit gestured. "We don't have pianos at this mortuary. We use keyboards." I followed his finger. The smallest, spindliest electronic keyboard I have ever seen rested on a steel stand. My heart sank. If the levels and features were not set exactly, no telling how the sound would turn out.

By now the room was full, and it was clear that I would not have an opportunity to test the instrument without an audience. I was not familiar with this model and the array of brightly colored buttons seemed to glow mockingly. *Why, oh why*, I lamented, *hadn't I double-checked about the piano situation. Had I known I'd be stuck with a keyboard, I could have gone in the night before to practice.* Worse luck, the tiny room forced me to play a scant five feet away from the front row of family members.

At least the neon alien knee was away from the audience, facing the wall and the casket.

The usher signaled me to take my seat at the keyboard and began the prelude music. With a sick feeling, I sat. I opened my music to the first song they had chosen. *Amazing Grace*. Oh, how I would need it.

I played the first measure. To my shock, a reverberating drum back beat began to accompany me! The sustain key was not set either and there was no manual pedal. The combined effect was a throwback to the seventies. I could almost hear the disc jockey yell, "EVERYBODY SKATE!" Thinking perhaps it might get better, I played measure two. Nope. I searched in vain for the percussion key. I had to turn it off! The family began to whisper and point. *Their accompanist was playing Disco Amazing Grace!*

Mortified, I slid off the bench and crouched, with as much dignity as any disco queen wearing green neon can muster, beneath rows of flowers, plants and cards from well-wishers and went in search of someone, *anyone,* who could fix this mess.

I poked my head in offices. No one. I looked at my watch. Three minutes until the minister entered the chapel, prayed and then expected me to play and sing, *sing!* the first song. I made a beeline for the back room with its metal preparation tables. *Bingo!* The owner had heard my dilemma over the loudspeaker and was bellowing that somebody had better get up there and fix those keyboard levels.

A chastened Donna Summer-by-default followed the Suit into Chapel A. He punched some buttons; I threatened to have him bound to one of those metal tables if I didn't have a sustain button when that keyboard was turned back on. He promised me there would be.

A peripheral glance at the family confirmed looks of wild relief. I began to play *Amazing Grace* again. Sans the drums. The minister emerged from the side room through red velvet curtains and bowed his head to pray.

And that's when it happened. The more I thought about *Disco Amazing Grace,* the funnier I thought it was. Stress combined with cold fear had made me unreasonably giddy. The harder I tried to get myself under control, the worse it got. My shoulders began to shake.

I turned my back to the audience and hoped they were the kind of folks who prayed with their eyes shut. I was about to lose it! I pinched myself. I tried to think the very saddest of thoughts. I wondered if my neighbors would ever still be my friends. A half-sob, half-snort escaped my lips and I prayed with all my heart that everyone thought I'd been overcome with grief.

I made it through the rest of the service by chewing the insides of my cheeks until they bled. As soon as the last of the family had filed past, just inches from me, I fled the scene.

All afternoon and all night I watched my neighbors' driveway. I wanted the chance to make things right, if such a thing were possible. At 10:45 that night, I finally saw their headlights pulling into the garage. Their phone rang approximately three seconds later.

"Hi. Melissa and Buddy? It's me." I refused to give my name. "Could I just come over for two minutes? There's something I have to do."

Dragging my poor husband (who had only heard the tale second-hand) along with me for moral support, I stood on their front porch, proffering a home-made cherry cheesecake and a stuttered apology.

To my surprise and eternal gratitude, they not only forgave me, they laughed. Hard! "We're so glad you went and got someone to fix the problem. We were all talking about how some people might have been too embarrassed to leave and just kept on playing!"

Too embarrassed to leave?! Were they *kidding?!*

They presented me with a gift certificate to thank me for singing and I played and sang *Amazing Grace* for them on their piano, the way that it *should* be played.

Whenever I need a reminder of such grace, I replay that movie in my mind.

I have other memories that run like the old 8 mm home movies. Fuzzy, a bit blurry even. But then I also have freeze frames. Snap shots. Clean, crisp still vivid shots. Captured images of other times, other places that remain imprinted on my heart forever. I like to call them *heart pictures*. Open your heart's album with me and leaf through its pages.

Some of the pictures will be funny, some poignant, some more striking than others. Just like those in mine.

The magical moment when my husband bent on one knee, having exchanged a plastic ring from a gumball machine for a wedding diamond, and asked me to marry him.

The first moment I held each of my seconds-old daughters, and the awed look on my husband's face as he witnessed these miracles.

Pictures of sleeping, rosy-cheeked infants. Snapshots of cake-smeared faces at first birthday parties. Memories of back packs, new school shoes and bright yellow buses, taking my babies on into the world.

Scripture says that Mary treasured all these things and pondered them in her heart. I bet she stored pictures in her heart's album of Jesus' first night in that smelly manger. The expressions on the faces of the men wise enough to bring her son gifts and worship Him.

Frozen images of Jesus playing kick the wineskin with the other boys in Nazareth. Of Jesus at twelve, in the temple, teaching those He'd helped create. Jesus and Joseph building a cabinet for the local pomegranate vendor. Of her son, hanging in agony on a cross.

Proverbs tells us, "As a man thinks in his heart, so is he." Apparently, it's important to be careful what we allow to be stored there. It's important that we learn to see with our heart too.

Once when Emmy was three, she spent the day with Grandma, all by herself. And the conversation, as it often does with children, turned to strange topics.

"Mimi" she queried, "Why don't you have some more babies since yours are all growed up?"

My mother explained that she was too old to be having babies. Emmy stared at her thoughtfully for a moment and then said, "Mimi, I don't see any old on you!"

We don't see flaws either when we look through hearts that love. Hearts that hold grace can't help but touch others with it. I often play hide-and-seek with my three precious girls. They have given me the honor of being "the goodest hider."

"I hope so," I tell them. "Because the most important thing to hide goes in your heart and it can't ever be lost." We talk about one of the first memory verses I ever learned. "Your word have I hid in my heart that I might not sin against you." They want to be good hiders too.

There are images, events, people, places, whose voices, sounds, sights, tastes, scents, I will never forget.

For example, if I close my eyes, I can hear the exact way my daddy read certain scripture verses or told certain illustrations from the pulpit.

When I went away to college, he and mother would often stay for Sunday worship at my local church. Daddy and I would try to guess what the preacher would say, filling in the blanks of the sermon outline in the bulletin. If we guessed wrong, daddy would mark across the questions - "Minus 2 - D+" We'd giggle a little while my circumspect mother tried to hush us. But mostly we made memories. My daddy and I. My mother and I. My sister and I. Precious heart pictures that don't need enlargements or negatives for clarity.

Cranking the handle on the old wooden ice-cream freezer

on the concrete steps of the back porch on sticky summer evenings.

Learning to make homemade bread with my mother on snowy, cozy afternoons.

Sunday School classes where teachers using flannel-graph boards and dusty chalkboards taught me lessons about life, about God, about the condition of my heart.

Bending over the couch with my sister to receive spankings after bouts of deliberate defiance. Then pondering with her how our parents, who otherwise seemed so smart, could say something as dumb as "This is going to hurt me more than it'll hurt you."

Playing Super Heroes and "Grown-up Office" with my little sister. Our desks were small aluminum and vinyl children's tables. We used Slinkys for telephones and we dreamed big dreams. I would write books. She would illustrate them. We'd be wealthy enough to take our parents with us on dream vacations.

Decorating shoe boxes with tin foil, glue, red construction paper hearts and candies before every school Valentine party.

Somedays, I long to go back. Because as Frederick W. Robertson wrote, "Home is the one place in all this world where hearts are sure of each other." Because we all desire a place to be loved unconditionally. I was fortunate enough for my childhood home to be one of those places. But to do so would be unfulfilling, for life is lived in fluid, moving moments. We must not try to make snapshots of moving pictures. There is a time for every season under heaven. We learn when to hang on, when to let go.

Sometimes, in the evening, three little urchins appear in our home. Sporting ballet costumes, gymnastic leotards, sunbonnets or old silk nightgowns, these three waif-like creatures dance, sing, tumble and entertain a captive audience of two. Here they are assured of standing ovations and high praise for their antics and their efforts.

Occasionally, we'll get restless, thinking of the other tasks that must be completed. Three faces turn to us and plead, "Oh, please stay for this part! The best thing is coming up!"

And so it is. God has promised that the best things in life are indeed yet to come.

I had a sixth grade teacher, Mr. Rothman, who was a mentor to me. He, along with another history my junior year of high school, made me want to teach. Mr. Rothman used to read to us by candlelight on rainy Friday afternoons from Edgar Alan Poe's short stories. The one I could never forget was called *The Tell-Tale Heart*.

The main character kills an old man because he hates the old man's deformed eye. When the police come knocking at his door to check on the reports of a scream from his apartment, he is so certain of pulling off the perfect crime that he pulls his chair over the exact spot on the floorboards where the body is buried!

As the police chat pleasantly with him, he begins to think he hears the beating of the old man's heart. It gets louder and louder until he screams out his confession. His conscience can no longer take the guilt. By the end of the story, there wasn't a sixth grader in the commons area who couldn't hear the thud of that hideous heart beating in their own eardrums! The candlelight reading of Poe became a tradition that I carry on with my own high-school students, twelve years later. It still makes quite the impression.

Scripture warns of the same lesson. "Above all, guard your heart, for it is the wellspring of life." "Man looks at the outward appearance, but God looks at the heart."

Maybe that's because knowing someone's heart tells us much about a person. Sometimes, our daughter Emily sits in the time-out chair until she thinks she is ready to listen. One afternoon, after she had been sitting for a while, I gave her permission to resume her play.

She turned around and looked at me. "No thanks, mommy, I'm not ready to listen yet."

It made me wonder if God doesn't desire such honesty from our hearts. As a child, after spending yet another day of second grade, standing in the corner for talking, I dreaded going home. Knowing my heart wasn't clean. Knowing the teacher would tell my parents. Knowing I'd be in trouble. . . . again.

I still sometimes dread having to go home and 'fess up to Greg about yet another impulse purchase.

But therein lies the sweet contradiction of home. Home is the one place you don't want to be when your heart isn't clean. It's also the only place you can think of to come clean.

Such acceptance at Home. Such Amazing Grace. Song writer Gloria Gaither wrote that "We can change the world inside our own houses." I believe that. And I think it starts with our hearts.

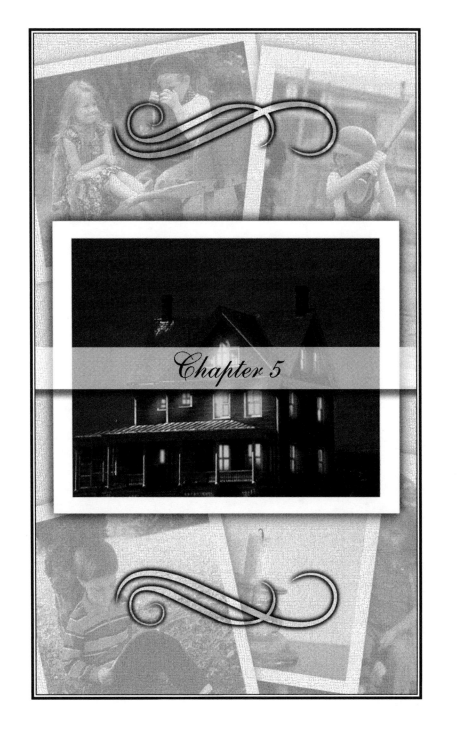

Chapter 5

## The Happy Box

*"Remember that happiness is a way of travel - not a destination."*
— Roy M. Goodman

or a long time we kept a red Tupperware sandwich box in an upstairs drawer. We affectionately dubbed it, *The Happy Box*. It didn't have value to anyone but us. It held loose change and the occasional dollar bill. When it was finally full, we'd treat ourselves to a movie at the dollar theatre and popcorn, a game of miniature golf or a pizza.

It gave mute plastic testimony to the known, but often forgotten fact that life can indeed be that simple. That there are life lessons, laughter lessons, love lessons, to be learned at home, during uncomplicated outings, on the playground, on the tire swing, at church camp.

A cacophonous din ricocheted across the playground, bouncing off monkey bars, sailing through swings and sliding down slides.

"Share!"

"It's my turn!"

"Watch me, Mommy!"

"Be careful, son."

Parents watched their precious children in the time honored dance of daring and caution. That fine line balance between parental shelter and letting go.

After a while, a little boy approached my then three-year-old daughter at the sandbox. He squatted down beside her. For a while they zoomed their dump trucks and sifted sand through toy sieves side by side.

Suddenly, the boy thought aloud. "I wonder what sand is made of?"

I scooted closer, anxious to hear this exchange.

Eden spoke with authority. "Oh, it's made of brown sugar with a little rocks, cinnamon and stuff mixed in. See?"

She held up a small cup and poured out its contents to demonstrate.

Satisfied that he knew the sand's components, he had one more question. "Well I wonder who thought sand up?"

"God," Eden replied.

A simple answer. Full of grace. Full of faith.

Last weekend I spoke at a women's retreat. That in itself was not unusual. But it was held at a genuine old-fashioned church camp, in fact, the same camp my daddy had attended as a boy.

Between sessions I strolled around the grounds on a beautifully warm, sunny, picturesque autumn day. First I slid down the slide. Then I hit the swings. Pumping my legs I soared higher and higher. I jumped off, groaning only slightly when my knees sent a prompt message to my brain. *You're thirty-something, not thirteen anymore.*

Next I walked until I encountered the tetherball courts. I hadn't even seen one of those since my sophomore year of high school, my last year of church camp. I batted the ball tied to the end of the fraying rope and walked on.

Then I saw them. Simple buildings with four corner posts,

a roof and crude redwood benches lining the concrete floor. Shelters, we used to call them. I sat down and time evaporated, washed away by a tide of memories. The hours I spent in such shelters memorizing scripture for team competitions, reading my Bible, dreaming adolescent dreams.

The musty smell of the mattresses and the dull ache of homesickness, writing letters home during rest time. The heat rising from uneven concrete slabs in front of the canteen. Reveling in the freedom to have a cold bottled pop and a Three Musketeers every single day for a week!

Competitive softball games. Bible skit night. Watching my best friend play Jezebel and throwing herself off the parapet. Watching teammates play the prophets of Baal and one, the role of Elijah, while the rest of us taunted their gods unmercifully. [My friend Patrick and I were a bit *too* good at taunting, our team leader lamented.] And all the while learning more than I knew at the time about the true God.

Adventuresome campers freezing the camp dean's boxers and running them up the flagpole before the sun was up. Doing the camp cheer, the camp clap and collectively complaining about camp food.

Showering in concrete showers with floor drains, crickets and Daddy Long Legs. Emerging shy and freshly scrubbed from the dormitory and walking hand in hand with some freshly shaved boy wearing his best jeans and some of his dad's Old Spice toward Chapel. Vespers, those evening services were called.

Campfire devotions. Whipperwills, hoot owls, cricket song, camp choruses floating upward. A vast variety of night sounds under the black canopy of sky with the lights of heaven smiling at us.

But most of all leaving. Exchanging addresses, promises to write and calling out, "See you next year!" Leaving fired-up for God. Ready to tackle my school, my friends, the world, for Him. Incredibly anxious to go home. And to go Home.

Like the word Christmas, the word home evokes instant images. Memories. For some of us wonderful. For others of us distorted. For still others, painful.

But regardless of our specific memories, a warm home shares certain features. The welcoming, tinkling sound of happy laughter and shared experiences. Thousands of impressions explode like so many shards of glass.

The best thing about home is its incredible ability to be a safe-house, a place of refuge. The spot to refuel for joy on the journey. Lucky was I to live in such a home.

When I was a little girl, I used to beg my father, a Christian church preacher, to become a Catholic priest so I could become a nun, leave the convent, meet a fabulous naval captain with seven children (but no wife) and then marry him and live out my dream of becoming like Maria in *The Sound of Music*. My father pointed out that religious questions aside, he was already married with two children, and that perhaps my dreams would need to be fulfilled in another way.

Undeterred, I remained charmed by Maria's joie de vivre, her love for all those children and her ability to carve joy (and clothing) out of old curtains. The romance with the Captain certainly didn't hurt either. So I continued to play at being Maria, roping my little sister and any available neighbors, dolls, or stuffed animals into the plot. I prayed for and dreamed about my future life's mate.

And God watched and smiled. While I was teaching high school in the town of Joplin, I tried out for, and won, the part of Maria in the Little Theatre production of *The Sound of Music*. For seven weeks of rehearsals and eight performances, I got to live my dream on stage.

On the same weekend, the following July, I married my own "Captain," a detective on the police force. I walked down the aisle on my father's arm to the strains of *The Wedding Processional from The Sound of Music.* I sang to my husband-to-be. The director of the previous summer's play came to my wedding, and several of my stage children showed up dressed in the costumes they had worn for my stage wedding. (The seven children? Let's just say that we have four beautiful girls and my husband thinks I should reduce my fantasy by three.)

I was recently greeted by my girls after returning from a weekend speaking engagement. After dispensing hugs and presents and receiving slobbery kisses and admiring priceless welcome home signs, my oldest pulled me aside.

"Mama, can I tell you something without hurting your feelings?"

Curious, I nodded my assent.

"I missed you lots and I'm glad you're back, but daddy was a little more fun than you. He let us stay in our jammies 'til noon and we didn't start cleaning *anything* up until an hour before daddy said you'd be home!"

I didn't know whether to cry at the comparison or laugh at my the look of consternation on my husband's face. I wisely chose to do neither and said merely that I was glad they'd had a good time. Point taken.

Too often I forget the message of the Happy Box. Like many of us, I spend too much of life being busy. We want life to slow down, but we wait for it to happen. That illusive peace and freedom can't be far away, we think. And so we end up living for the next big raise; next summer's exotic vacation; the new furniture to arrive; that promised promotion. We wallow in "what ifs" and "if onlys."

When I am living this way, sometimes I feel cheated.

Instead of digging into life's treasure chest and unearthing a handful of treats, I end up falling into the busyness, all the way at the bottom and then spend all of my time clawing my way to the top, where I imagine daylight and organization are waiting. Not unlike the feeling I had as a child after a visit to the dentist when I'd paw through the chest and come out with an ugly plastic slug instead of a coveted ring.

Slugs creep into Happy Boxes when we are so busy living that we forget to carve out sacred places in life.

Remember that sometimes life is about staying in your jammies 'til noon, stuffing your mug of cocoa with marshmallows, relishing a hand-written letter from an old friend. Monday Night Football. A productive day at work. A long walk, munching apples, reveling in the Autumn breeze. A good night's rest. Being thankful for a bill which was smaller than you had originally feared. Exercising grace and becoming thankful for that which is daily extended to us.

But being "happy" is not about fulfilled dreams (though I've had many). Nor is it about keeping perfect order in the business world and on the home front. It is about cherishing. It is about contentment. It is about squeezing each drop out of life.

As the poet Emily Dickinson wrote, "Life only happens once." And that is what makes it so sweet.

The thing about life is that you have to show up for it. *All* of it. We do not get to pick and choose. Existence cannot be mistaken for *having* a life. Pulling the covers up over our head and letting time creep by is a poor choice.

As I grow older, I realize that time creeps only in seasons of grief, and even then, only in our own subjective worlds. For in the grand scheme of things, time marches. It grows wings and flies. Scripture tells us that God does not tell time in the same manner that we do. "With the Lord a day is like a thousand years, and a thousand years are like a day." (II Peter 3:8b) In fact, I'm not so sure that He even has a clock.

So what then are we to do with our short time on this earth? My daddy answered my question by loving life. No one was sorrier to leave or more ready to go than he was, when cancer finally stamped his out. He had lived every day like it was the gift we all know it to be in our better moments.

"Cinso," he loved to tell me, "Live like you'll die tomorrow; die knowing you'll live forever." I think he gave me the point of happiness and the key to Home.

The Happy Box is defunct now. Having served its purpose, it retired, a broken, dishwasher-warped icon. But we always make sure there is something to stand in for its message.

A Tupperware sandwich box, a hay-strewn manger, a splintery cross, a nail-scarred hand. A God who loves us enough to save our tears. Collectors of happiness, all.

Chapter 6

## Porch Swings

*"'Stay,' is a charming word in a friend's vocabulary."*
— Louisa May Alcott

*U*sed to be that people built wide front porches with porch swings and rockers, hanging baskets and wide steps that fairly sang, "Stay a while." Nowadays, people build back decks with high privacy fences.

I think I'm more of a front porch person myself.

My husband and I conducted a great deal of our courtship on a front porch swing. When we got married, we moved it to a tree branch in our yard, since our first home was porchless. When we moved to our current home, the old porch swing stayed behind. But one year on our anniversary, my husband graciously purchased and hung another porch swing for me. It sways on our wraparound porch, a testament of love, a reminder of simpler times and gracious living.

When friends to come to call, we often find our way out to the porch for homemade icecream, lemonade and visits on the wide wooden rockers and of course, the porch swing.

A surprising amount of living can be done on a porch swing. Various important conversations, big and small, have taken place on a porch swing.

Before my husband was my husband, he told me of his desire to accept Christ and be baptized while sitting on a porch swing.

Our oldest daughter convinced me to let her get her ears pierced (and convinced me to pierce mine too!) while sitting on a porch swing.

Emmy and Ellie have swinging contests and read-a-thons on the porch swing.

It was on our porch swing that a dear friend told me she was expecting again after her miscarriage.

Summer evenings will often find my husband and I on the porch swing, eating peanuts in the shell, drinking coca cola and talking about important world issues. The downstairs toilet is leaking again. The baby said her first word today. Can you believe next month will be October already? What do you want for Christmas? Let me tell you what I want for Christmas. What's that noise? May I have new curtains for the family room? Why would you need curtains for the family room? Guess how many papers I have to grade? Guess how much I love you!

Looking ahead, I can almost see our little girls, perched on the threshold of womanhood, sitting on the porch swing with their future dates (the last age their dad gave them on when that will be is twenty-five) while Greg spies on them from the dining room window and flicks the porch light when it's time to come in.

I've read that porch swings are making yet another big comeback, and I'm glad. Erma Bombeck wrote of their value in her September 22, 1994 column, *At Wit's End*. She described for a generation who had practically skipped the porch phenomenon what such a place was.

> It was a place that had a swing that squeaked. There was a roof over it so that when it rained you could swing back and forth and listen to the sound of it falling and smell the fresh earth. Kids left their bicycles and wagons on it so people wouldn't trip over them on the sidewalk in the darkness.

After dinner, parents had their coffee on the porch to watch the parade of people taking walks. Sometimes they stopped to get caught up on the news of the neighborhood.

I think of this every time I land on my neighbor's porch, or she on mine, to drop off a pie, some cookies, a piece of misdirected mail, a soccer schedule or just to shoot the breeze.

I guess part of the appeal of porch swing living is its retreat value from a world that doesn't have time for leisure. I, along with a growing number of others, have an insatiable desire for something more. And that something more is something less. I want to recapture my life. Make my time my own.

To do instead of watch.

To live instead of spectating.

To be instead of rushing.

I think Erma made a strong case when she thought the path to such desires might lead to a front porch.

That desire seems to be cyclical in history. As a history teacher and history lover, I am fascinated by the things, people and lessons of the past.

The resilient spirit of the people who lived through the Great Depression make that era one of the most intriguing. Like Erma Bombeck, I too have heard some older folks talk about the Great Depression with such fondess it makes me sick I missed it!

An October 1932 editorial in *The Ladies Home Journal,* makes reference to the frenzied spending and rampant materialism of the roaring twenties (sound familiar?), the subsequent stock market crash and the contrasting world of economic depression.

"There is a prosperity of living which is quite as important as prosperity of the pocketbook. . . .Where we were specialists in spending, we are becoming specialists in living."

It's still good counsel for today. *Specialists in living.* That's a kind of specialist I would like to become. Afterall, isn't that what abundant living is all about? It's a hard task though, as I realize, stricken with guilt as Emmy follows me around trying to gain my attention as I rush from dryer to stairs, to stove to dishwasher and back. "Mommy!" she demands. "Quit going everywhere!" And when I am at last still, her chubby arms grasp my knees tightly and I am blessed.

On especially hectic days, I am frantic to become more adept at this simplistic living business. (I almost said, a simplistic liver, but that doesn't conjure up quite the right picture, does it?). But then I realize that to be in hot pursuit of the simple life is a contradiction.

What we need is Jesus' brand of porch swing living. "Come to me all you who are weary and I will give you rest?" Rest. True fulfillment. Porch swing living recalls Jesus' gracious invitation to "learn the unforced rhythms of grace." {Matthew 11:29, *The Message*}

Isn't that what the world craves more than money? Even those who rush to be the next millionaire, claim that they want the money to pay off bills, travel, slow down, quit rushing, help others. Do we have to have millions to do that? I wonder.

Recent surveys show that 80% of women and 60% of men would take a cut in pay in order to spend more time with their families. Gratitude journals and books on simplistic living are making a comeback. Country Inns and Bed & Breakfasts have more appeal than ever. Rural real estate is booming. The cities empty on the weekends.

What can we learn from porch swing living? There's little that can't be fixed with WD40, love or attention. That a smattering of clouds or a sprinkling of stars against the wrong side of heaven's tablecloth is glorious. That caterpillars and walking sticks are fascinating creatures.

That there's not a much better place to curl up with your toddler and read. To coax confidences out of your adolescent. To snuggle with your mate. To reclaim the time.

If you're swinging in a porch swing, there's not a lot else you can do. Languish. Linger. Welcome. Chat. Read. Doodle. Relax. Lost arts, really. Done any of those things lately? If not, maybe it's time to renew the time-honored ritual of porch sitting.

After the supper dishes are done, go out and sit on the porch swing and watch the kids play. Enjoy the clinking of icecubes and the swish of lemonade against tall glasses on hot summer days. Bundle up with afghans and thick mugs of cocoa brimming with marshmallows on cool autumn evenings. Write a letter by hand

Pray, read your Bible. Talk to God, or better yet, listen to Him.

Porch swing living invites. It doesn't hurry. It can't rush. It restores and refreshes. Rare commodities these days.

To engage in porch swing living is to open your life to others. My poor only-child husband is often confounded by the fact that our doorbell is apt to ring and people he has never seen stand on the other side.

"We heard your wife speak at a retreat and after all those stories she told about rats and remodeling while you restored this old place, we were just so curious. She said we could stop by!"

A member of our church or Sunday School class drops by for a few moments just to see how things are going. To rejoice with us about something. To pray for us. To laugh.

Greg is astounded. I am delighted.

Better than a phonecall, to me, is a drop-in visit. A chance to connect. To talk to a breathing human being instead of an answering machine, an automated teller, a credit-card swiping machine.

Agatha Christie wrote, "I like living. I have sometimes been wildly, despairingly, acutely miserable, racked with sorrow, but through it all I still know quite certainly that just to be alive is a grand thing."

The Apostle Paul echoed this sentiment. "I have learned the secret of being content in every situation."

Learned it. It takes practice, that's for sure. Life will not and cannot always consist of porch swing moments. That wasn't promised to us and it would make for a dull life anyway. But some moments will be, if we look for them.

Contentment doesn't come easily. But then, does anything worthwhile? Contentment in every situation. Amazing. Being happy after you've already gotten everything you want doesn't count. Counting your blessings does.

Try it. Get out the old hymnal and sing it. Write down three things for which you are thankful every night before you go to sleep. Then thank God for them. I've found that usually, three things aren't nearly enough. I have life, I have breath, I have a porch swing.

And the God who formed me, flung the stars in the heavens and counts the hairs on my head, knows me. He knows my name. As Elisabeth Elliot wrote, "What matters to me matters to Him and that changes my life." Is it changing yours?

Heed the call of the porch swing. It's rest for a weary soul. God has always advocated living over busyness. Motives over appearances. Authenticity over riches.

Like each snowflake, each autumn leaf, no two moments are exactly the same. And they will never come again. Make some of them porch swing moments.

When's the last time you've thought it was grand to be alive? It's even better knowing you'll live forever one day.

That invitation is the sweetest of all to share. Stressed out this week? This month? This lifetime?

Then maybe it's time to tear down the fences, get out on the porch, water the geraniums and swing your feet.

Chapter 7

Main Street

*"The great street of the city was of pure gold, like transparent glass."*
— Revelation 21:21

There aren't many folks left that grew up with an actual Main Street. Cruising on Friday nights. Icecream sodas at the fountain bar. Juicy burgers and crisp fries drowned in catsup in a back booth, long before cholesterol was a big health issue. Drug stores that sold everything from Band-Aids, cough medicine and greeting cards to wrapping paper, hair ribbons and big pink wads of bubble gum.

Dirt thoroughfares trampled by horses and buggies that gave way to asphalt traveled by automobiles. The center of action. The pulsebeat of life in a small town. General stores with wooden rockers and huge wooden cigar Indians. Bright bolts of cloth and apothecary jars filled with hard candies competed for space with barrels of soda crackers and sacks of flour. Even the old tin advertising signs and food cans are collectibles now. Memories, sought after by those who want to recapture the ease and intimacy of a slower-paced, familiar way of life.

I'm not old enough to remember all of that, but I too yearn for the memories passed down to me. I live in a town big enough to boast a McDonalds, Walmart, Taco Bell and even a shopping mall. But it's also small enough that we frequently run into my former high school students, our friends, work colleagues and fellow church members. We stop and exchange trivial pleasantries. *How's it goin'? Hear the parade got cancelled? Are you out here for the ball game? Good to see you.* Small things, but precious.

A town small enough for a drycleaner who prayed for me on exam days during graduate school. For quaint antique shops that still welcome browsers. A drive-through bank teller who knows that I always need three suckers, all the same flavor, please. A grocery store cashier who greets us by name. A donut shop where I can ask for "the usual." A town where if people see your name in the paper, they mail you the clipping and show up at your book signings, little theatre plays and school events.

There's a central ball-field where parents and kids gather and visit, sharing stories, runs batted in, stale popcorn and sweet conversation on hot summer evenings under the dusty twilight and bright lights of Little League.

It's a place where the postman knows I favor the stamps with berries on them and how much it costs to mail a packet of pictures overseas. Where the lone policeman knows to watch for my van and graciously remind me to slow down and The Red Onion Cafe knows our favorite table. A town where people still put their hands over their hearts when they see the flag and whose elementary students open each school day with the national anthem. A place where a local television station's slogan is: "Your hometown news: where local news comes first." It's a hometown which boasts places where people recognize my face, know my family and realize that we have lives and names, not just identification numbers.

Ideally such a sense of hometown community is a preview of heaven. If you watch and listen for the small miracles, a Main Street mentality can be yours too.

The only thing that bothered me greatly about our impending move from town into the semi-boondocks was that my daddy had never been in this new old house. I wanted to be able to picture him around our table, laughing with the grandkids on the floor, eating a bowl of homemade icecream on the porch. But cancer was clearly claiming my fifty-six years young father, and I knew there was a possibility he wouldn't live that long.

I mailed my parents a videotape of the property and the outside of the rambling structure just days before daddy's death. On tape, I acted as tour guide while my husband filmed. I pointed out the wide wrap-around veranda and gestured grandly toward the pond and the fifty-two cows that was to be our beautiful view. (As a city girl, my previous experience with cows had been limited to the kind in shrink-wrapped styrofoam, all ready for the grill). I walked down the lane to the mailbox and teasingly reminded my folks that I wanted this box stuffed with letters from home.

The tape ended with me holding my swollen, nine months pregnant belly and pleading: "Daddy, hold on a little longer. Baby Ellie really wants you to hold her and I want you to see this old house. I love you." When I made a flying visit home to St. Louis three days before daddy's death, we sang, talked, hugged and cried for hours. One of the things I showed him was my "dream house notebook". I walked him through an imaginary tour of the inside of the house as well.

Three days after that visit, baby Ellie was born on her due date at 8:12 p.m.; twelve hours later daddy died. When she was three days old, we made the five hour journey for daddy's visitation and funeral. It was indescribably hard.

Moving day had already been scheduled for July 29, on our anniversary. Baby Ellie was nineteen days old.

Eleven months after we'd moved, we sat at the ballpark one summer evening, watching our oldest daughter, Eden, make her first base hit, and then run home, courtesy of her teammates. You'd have thought it was her 40th homerun. Cheering wildly, I turned to my mother sitting on the bleachers beside me and said, "How daddy would've loved to be here tonight." We were pensive and hurtfully lonely for a moment, then determinedly went on with life by discussing the latest adventure involving the loveable wreck of a farmhouse we'd purchased. (If I remember correctly, it was the third time the dining room ceiling had fallen in.)

The game ended and we greeted Eden with whoops and high fives. As we jubilantly left the diamond and headed to our car, a woman followed us. "Wait," she said. "I couldn't help hearing some of your conversation. Did you buy the old Oliver place?"

I nodded.

"My daughter went to college with you. She told me your maiden name was Sigler. Was your dad Don Sigler?"

I nodded again as she continued. "I used to live in that house. Grew up there. Your daddy was good friends with my brother and they played basketball in college together."

I was so thrilled I hugged her! I explained that I had been inexplicably sad that daddy had never been in my house.

"I'm sure he's been in the kitchen and dining room for sure. In fact, I believe he came to dinner a few times."

My eyes filled with tears and I thanked her for that gift. An answer to prayer in an unexpected way, in an unexpected place. On Main Street, so to speak. Daddy had been in my house afterall, nearly forty years earlier. Pieces of heaven.

You never know what you'll discover on Main Street. The

promise of such tidbits made the local post office the gathering place for my husband's father in their hometown. He tells me that mail collection took a minimum thirty minutes. Men stood in clumps, slumped against the walls, swapping news and talking politics. It was a town that boasted fireworks over the lake on Independence Day, outdoor summer concerts and the friendly rivalry of the annual barbershop quartet competition.

Small towns seem to invite chatting, browsing, lingering. I began my teaching career in one such small town. During my summer walks there, I always passed the grain and feed mill. I eagerly anticipated the waving and tipping of hats from the group of weathered, relaxed, friendly farmers who congregated on its porch during their morning break.

Every Labor Day weekend, the town hosted its annual Community Days Celebration. Everyone turned out for craft booths, a peek at the retired fire engines, funnel cakes and the county's largest barbeque. Such events hurtled me backward in history to the picturesque scenes of my parents' hometown. On my childhood visits there, it seemed that white churches with steeples dotted the patchwork pieces of farmland like a giant quilt whose stitches were made with Pixie Sticks. Standing in front of any one of those churches, I was instantly transported to a time of church socials, box suppers and Sunday School picnics.

Current real estate trends prove I'm not alone in this fantasizing - the move is on from the suburban to the rural. *Recapturing the charm of neighborhood picnics, back fence fraternizing, and the illusive feel of Main Street belonging, just might be easier in small town America,* goes the thinking.

Main Street is still the place to be to find out the latest news, to people watch. It is a gathering place. A meeting spot with icecream cones by the fountain in front of the newspaper office. Of course if you're not spending time on Main Street, you might miss such things. Even more so, if the street is gold.

A Main Street Mentality only happens when we spend time with people; wave our hands in greeting; smile at passersby; get to know the kids in our neighborhood; visit on a neighbor's porch; carol in the snow; express genuine interest in the answer to "How's it goin'?" It develops by caring about the weather for the sake of Farmer Kettleman's corn crop. Discussing the stock market closings with Jim Hutton who works in a brokerage.

Sympathizing about the pain of Mrs. Johnson's appendectomy scar. Rejoicing over Jean Allen's first real estate sale. Attending the fourth baby shower in a week. Stopping at a curbside lemonade stand. Buying a candybar to support the local high school band and six boxes of Girl Scout cookies every Spring.

Jesus knew this, of course. It's why He always made time to spend time with people. To hang out with His friends. It's why we sometimes read scripture only to find Him doing something surprising with His time. Hosting impromptu picnics. Fishing. Catching a refreshing nap during a thunderstorm. Going to parties. Resting by a well in the center of town. Playing with the children. Attending a wedding reception. Having late night coffee with an important city official.

Sometimes circumstances draw people together no matter how large the community. Tragedies, illness, crimes, natural disasters. We remember to forget how different we all are and to pursue common goals.

And sometimes, God allows us glimpses of what will be. Scripture says that this earth is His footstool (Isaiah 66:1) This is an awesome planet. If this is just the footstool, I want to see the couch! The throne room! The Maker of Footprints!

There are many things about this earth that are wonderful. Glorious, even, in their own way. Sunsets. A baby's first cry. The great ocean roar caged in the delicate pink of a seashell's ear. The twists and turns of a river. The intoxicating thrill of first love. Gnarled and twisted hands still clasped in love after sixty years of marriage. Sunrise at the Grand Canyon. The Eiffel tower at dusk. Westminster Abbey. Carriage rides in the snow. The endless slap of the waves on the coasts. The pristine white froth stirred up by the ferry boats going across the English Channel. The crackling glow of a campfire and the warmth of the stories shared and memories made there. The traffic, the colorful storefronts, the humanity, the diversity, the commraderie of Main Street.

How glorious will be the Main Street of heaven! "The great street [Main Street] of the city was of pure gold, like transparent glass." (Revelation 21:21) The twelve gates of its entrance are each made of a single pearl (those poor oysters)!

If we work it right, life here offers the chance to practice life on that golden Main Street. It's a beautiful street. A permanent street with no potholes. A safe street - "On no day will its gates ever be shut, for there will be no night there. . . .Nothing impure will every enter it, nor will anyone who does what is shameful or deceitful, but only those whose names are written in the Lamb's book of life." (Revelation 21:25;27) Imagine the grandeur!

Even better, imagine a city Main Street where jealousy, hurt feelings, and selfishness are non-existent. Where there are no time constraints. You can pick Apostle Paul's brain about his exploits and preaching style. You can ask Lot if he still likes salt on his french fries. Find out if Noah found it hard to build an ark in the face of ridicule or to continue preaching for so many years with only seven converts, all of them family.

You could check with Rahab to see if her heart beat faster when the city officials came to her door late at night, asking her if she'd seen any spies lately. You may question Mary, the mother of God, about what she wrote in His baby book.

Finally our knowledge will be complete. No more seeing through a glass darkly. We'll know who *really* shot JFK. We'll understand why a spouse suffered with an agonizing disease. We'll comprehend the reason why we didn't land that dream job. We'll understand the loss of a child, taken from us too soon.

But best of all, we'll have eternity to stroll down Main Street arm in arm, hand in hand, with the One Who Loves Us Best. To talk with Him over chocolate malts at Heaven's Manna Rock Cafe. We can do it forever if we want to.

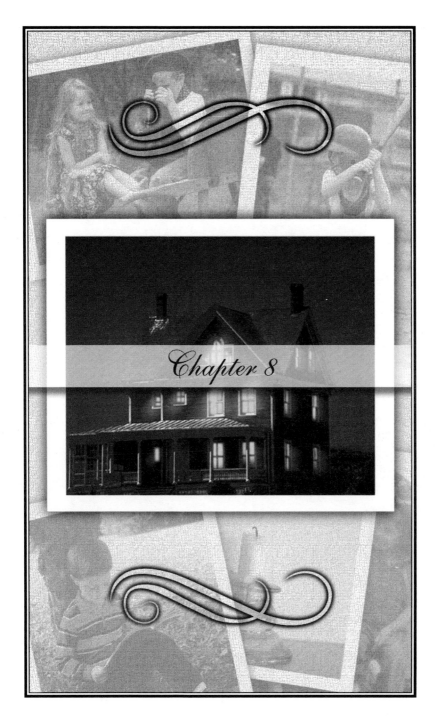

Chapter 8

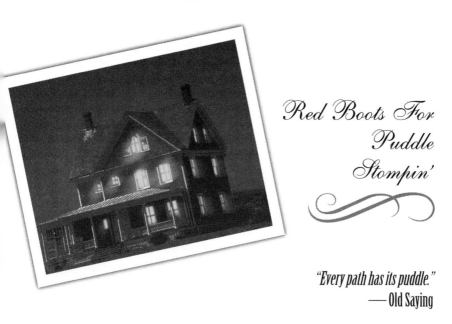

# Red Boots For Puddle Stompin'

*"Every path has its puddle."*
— Old Saying

*S*omewhere between ages three and thirty, I lost it. I traded my spirit of adventure for a spirit of admonition. I first noticed it the day I had all three of my little girls in tow and stopped at the mall to run an errand. A light rain had fallen that morning, and small puddles, filled with oily rainbows, had gathered along the curb and sidewalk. My oldest daughter, Eden, was gleefully raking her feet across the concrete and jumping in each one with wholehearted abandon.

"Eden," I scolded, "Stop that, you'll ruin your new school shoes." Her face fell. "Sorry, mom," she responded in the sorriest little voice I'd ever heard. Where she saw delight, I found irritation. Where she saw opportunity, I voiced negativity.

What finally shamed me was the obvious enjoyment of passersby as they watched her play.

I'd forgotten that although puddles are messy and sometimes result in painful accidents, they can also be occasions of great joy. Or at least occasions of character.

This has been a week of puddles for me, writing-wise. I sent a piece called, "The Power of a Daddy" to a parenting magazine and they wrote back, "This is not a subject suited to the needs of our magazine." *Right. How silly of me to have sent out such a query to the wrong market.* (Thank goodness a different magazine publication picked it up!)

I sent a piece entitled, "25 Ways to Love Your Husband," and the editor wrote back asking if I could prove any of them worked. Sigh. *Sometimes accepting the existence of puddles is difficult.*

Puddles happened when I was a single mother, left alone with a sixteen-month old daughter, heartbroken and wondering what would make my minister-husband walk out on a commitment. Alone, I had more outgo than income. More deadlines than time. More demands than energy. More requests than patience. But I learned that God is indeed my Husband and my Maker.

Puddles formed smaller, irritating pools when my sister and brother-in-law lived next door to me, waiting for my marriage to Greg so they could move into the "Big House" that I vacated. But we also shared the sweetest of times, laughing, renting late night movies and hanging my sister's pictures on the wall as fast as I took mine down.

Puddles happened when my father's cancer advanced militantly, stealing him away from us too quickly. But we learned that miracles still happen. And when the time for that miracle vanished, we learned that God is still God in the midst of unspeakable pain.

Puddles happened this week as I sat down in my dining room and tried to write, listening to the plumbers noisily and expensively fixing a collapsed drain. The puddles grew larger a few hours later when I began sweeping up the mess and encountered a snake in our bathroom. . . . and ran! [Thank you to my capable husband who drove home like a maniac and to my ever-faithful neighbor, Buddy, who beat the snake unconscious while my husband held it down with a shovel.]

Puddles happen when we are turned down for that

promotion, when are dreams are deferred, when our calendars crunch, when our health fails, when a betrayal makes us feel sucker-punched.

Puddles happen when a bride becomes a widow and faces that utterly lonely obscenity of one plate, one fork, one glass, one napkin where there were once two. Going to church and finding that all around are pews filled with couples. Having to go to the movies alone. My friend Julie experienced that at age twenty-six. My mother tearfully accepted that coupleless title at fifty-six. Both must spend some time slogging through potholes without their life's partner.

Puddles happen when our worlds break, either as a result of our own poor choices, or by circumstance. Gordon MacDonald in his book, *Rebuilding Your Broken World,* makes two observations about learning from such puddles. First, virtually every major player in the Bible had a broken world experience; most grew from that experience. Secondly, whether suddenly or gradually, eventually broken-world people get around to the concept of hope. *Could there be life after this brokenness?* And mercifully, that is when God does His best work.

Puddles happened when we decided, happily, that three girls were enough busyness and joy for one lifetime and we packed up the rattles, strollers, baby and maternity clothes and strollers for a garage sale.

Then God decided He had other plans and blessed us with a glorious fourth surprise. . . for thirteen weeks. One day, the heartbeat was not present. That which we had greeted with wonderment and then growing elation had died. Baby Elayna Jo.

Once again, my world was rocked. Stoned with deafening questions and met with staggering silence. I was angry. How could God give us such a sweet gift and then refuse to allow us to open the package?

I had not yet known this child in the sense that I know my other children. I had not yet held her, kissed her, diapered her. But oh, I had loved her just the same. I breathed for her, carried her. We were knit together sharing the same body, and for a while, the same heart.

But He was there, drawing near to my grief, waiting for me to come to my senses long enough to receive His comfort.

When we really stop to think of it, we realize that *this* day, *this* moment, *this* experience will never come again. Life is frail, fleeting, fragile. And wonderful.

To believe this is not a naive head-in-the-sand approach to life. It is to acknowledge that God is in control, no matter what happens. It is choosing to live life in a state of hopefulness. I learned yet again that for the believer, our good-byes are not without that hope. Did we not have the promise of meeting our loved ones yet again, the rancid hopelessness that follows death would be permanent. The apostle Paul reminded us that we may grieve, but not as those who have no hope.

> *If I can endure for this minute*
> *whatever is happening to me,*
> *No matter how heavy my heart is,*
> *Or how dark the moment may be —*
> *If I can but keep on believing*
> *What I know in my heart to be true,*
> *That darkness will fade with the morning*
> *And that this will pass away too—*
> *Then nothing in life can defeat me*
> *For as long as this knowledge remains*
> *I can suffer whatever is happening*
> *For I know God will break all the chains*
> *That are binding me tight in the darkness*
> *And trying to fill me with fear—*
> *For there is no night without dawning*
> *And I know that my morning is near.*
> *~Unknown*

Maybe you've noticed that the people you learn the most from and want to be around the most are not the people with perfect lives. They are not people who have been sheltered from every crisis. They are not those whose lives appear, at least on the surface, to be flawless.

Instead, they are those who exhibit resilience, grace and faith. Those who have wobbled, been knocked down, but never knocked out. They have refused to quit. They have illuded bitterness. They have character, experience, hope. They stand by your side in the tough times and cheer, "You can make it!"

They acknowledge the heart-rendering reality of pain. The breathtaking, soul threatening doubt that occurs when cold reality collides with your warm expectations, drenching your family, your community, your very being.

But then in the compassionate voice of one who has been there, they gently refuse to allow you to wallow in self-pity. They encourage, pull, prod and expect. They remind you that life goes on and despite everything, it is good.

Perhaps in my effort to *care* for my children, I have too often been the wet blanket.

"Be careful."

"Ugh! Stay out of that mud!"

"Not tonight, we need to pick up the house and get ready for the week."

And while the mother-instinct in me longs to pray that my children will be spared any pain, every heartache, every uncertain doubt, I know that would not be wise.

Pain is unavoidable. If you live life, you will experience pain. There are no exemptions. So it is better that I pray they will have the strength, wisdom and grace to carry them through and emerge even stronger on the other side.

For balance, their daddy wisely gives them the gift of

being less care-full. He is a reminder of joy. He wants us all to work hard and then play like nobody's business!

Of course, much depends on your perspective. For example, to a worm, it's a lot more relaxing to spend the day digging tunnels in the dirt than to spend the day fishing.

The difference lies in whether we see puddles only as ugly messes, violating our schedules, splashing mud on our best laid plans, drenching our dreams with random wetness, or whether we can see grace there too.

There's no escape from puddles, to be sure. They're a fact of life. But home can change our perspective on what we do with them. Stomp, splash, splatter. Joy. Brokenness. Hope. Perhaps the best way to deal with puddles is to jump right in, red boots and all.

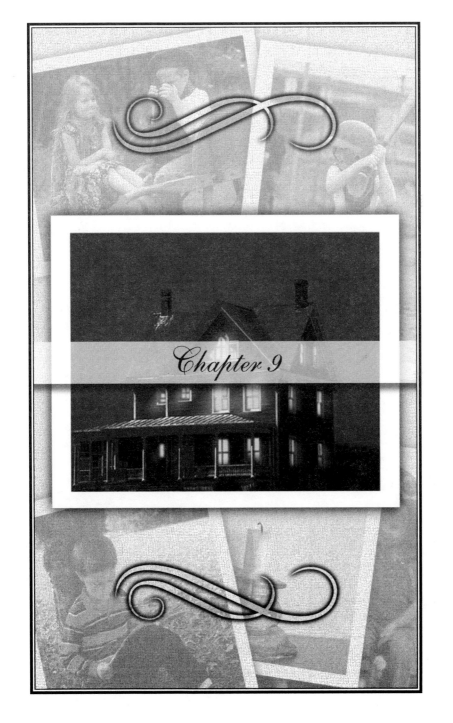

Chapter 9

## Daddy and the Roller Coasters

*"No eye has seen, no ear has heard, no mind has conceived what God has prepared for those who love him."*
— I Corinthians 2:9

*I* rode my first roller coaster at the age of three, so I'm told. I rode three times, buckled in next to my daddy until the man in charge of the yardstick noticed I was too short, and spoiled our fun. No matter. It was the beginning of a lifelong love of those thrilling rides.

To this day, it's the first place I head at any amusement park. When the ride's over, I climb out, run around to the gate and ride again. I especially love the slow days when others aren't waiting for their turn and the engineer says, "All those who want to ride again, stay aboard." And for those of us who love those rides, the heights are thrilling.

The problem is, we've become so accustomed to such thrills that we're irritated, self-righteously indignant even, about the dips. The lows. The trials. The endless moments of mundane. Sitting in traffic. Waiting in line. Ho hum. Sorting socks. Mowing the lawn. Making the beds. Bending. Stretching. Stooping. Reaching.

It seems that we wait in line 35 minutes for just 2 minutes of fun.

But then, on some days, there is climbing. Soaring. The glory of the heights. Oh the thrills! Tummy tripping. Teeth clenching. Exhilarating. What a view! What a life!

And then it happens. We begin the descent. Hurtling toward the bottom of a dragon of steel in a car that now seems rickety and inadequate for the job. Sometimes we plunge so fast that it knocks us breathless.

We dread those dips because the climb back upward to those heights seems so steep. Dangerous. We forget that the only view lies at the top. That the climb makes us appreciate the view all the more.

Dips are necessary for the thrill, but the sheer contrast can make us dizzy. We trade the pain of childbirth for the miraculous wails of a writhing, perfect newborn. We exchange the initial excitement of signing up for our dream job for the rewards of hard slogging through the trenches. We temper the giddy, physical thrill of courtship with the deeper blending of souls who make love and make love last.

Roller coaster lovers are those who like to go the distance. Never quit. They sign up to be test riders for the newest, highest thrillers, because they remember the thrill of the ending even before it begins. They are wise and they know that the dips seem scarier in the dark. In the tunnels. At night.

And they know that light always follows. When you burst into the light, such fears seem laughable.

They understand that heights and drops are inseparable. They know from long experience that you don't get one without the other. The thrill of the climb is wrapped in the scary safety of the plunge that follows. You just have to watch for the signs.

I once heard my daddy tell this story from the pulpit. Three little old ladies were riding in a car. One was driving, the other two rode in the backseat. Along one long stretch of interstate, a policeman pulled the car over, not too far from a posted speed limit sign.

"Ma'am. I'm sorry to have stopped you, but you're going

way too fast. This is a 60 MPH zone, and you were doing 80!"

Respectfully, the petite white-haired driver replied, "Well, officer, I just saw a black and white sign back there, and it read '80'."

The officer thought for a moment and then understanding lit up his face. "This is *Highway* 80, ma'am. That sign tells the road number, not the speed limit."

Then he noticed the white-knuckled, pale ladies in the backseat. Leaning in the window he queried, "What's the matter ladies?"

After a long minute, one of them choked out, "Well officer, we just got off Highway 125!"

We don't want to mistake the signs either. It'd be a shame to confuse the thrills here with those that are yet to be. Beloved author and philosopher C.S. Lewis once said, "Enjoy the inns along the way, but don't mistake them for home."

Keeping the pleasures of this life in the proper perspective help make the dips easier to handle. As my friend and minister, Sherm Nichols, says, "Nothing is so hard to come down off of gracefully as your high horse." Dreams of self-importance are such animals.

A few months ago, a major publisher called our house asking to speak with me about a book I was working on. I was thrilled and tried desperately to keep the elation out of my voice and be the calm professional I knew I could be.

Big mistake if you're in the house alone, dressed in a wool bathrobe, hair dripping wet and your toddler and preschooler are upstairs unsupervised.

I tried to focus on the conversation, but Emmy's insistent voice was piercing. "Mom! Come up here! Help me! Come see what Ellie's doing—you won't like it!"

I took the phone into another room, trying to ignore her plea just until I could gracefully get off the phone.

I had seriously considered hiding out in the van in order to finish this important conversation, when an ear-splitting yell pierced the stairwell. "MOMMY COME UP HERE NOW! ELLIE'S TRYING TO WIPE ME!"

I raced upstairs, phone tucked under my chin, trying desperately (and failing) to signal Emily that she should pipe down. The sight was better than comical. Emmy, who's potty-trained, was seated on the throne. Ellie, who is not, was valiantly trying to scoot Emmy off the seat, wad of toilet paper in hand, so she could wipe her big sister just as she had seen me do. Down from the heights with a thud.

I bought new shoes today and left the box in the family room floor. The baby picked it up and put it on her head, stumbling through the room like a drunken elf. I laughed at her antics and she laughed back with the insistent delirium of babydom.

We're a lot alike in that sense, I guess. Easily entertained. But every now and then, the box isn't enough. We crave bigger and better. I've noticed that happens more often as you get older. We're longing for home.

I suppose all of do that at times. We stumble around caught up in the box-like pleasures of this life, thinking *perhaps this is all there is.* We forget that there's more. Roller coaster heights. Thrills, dips, climbs. Forever.

When I am tempted to be too easily entertained by this world's toys, I try to remember what legacy I want to leave—a legacy that loved roller coasters. I want those who know me to say, "God was her passion."

And then I remember that those who are passionate about God wear aprons. Confused? Think about it. Waiters were aprons. Mothers wear aprons. Servants wear aprons. Jesus fashioned a towel into an apron right before he knelt and washed the dirty feet of his weary disciples. Sometimes I am certain that the ability to don an apron is vital to leading a fulfilled life.

The comedian Gilda Radner had this to say about the roller coaster factor in life: "I wanted a perfect ending. Now I've learned the hard way that some poems don't rhyme and some stories don't have a clear beginning, middle and end. Life is about not knowing, having to change, taking the moment and making the best of it, without knowing what is going to happen next. Delicious ambiguity."

Delicious ambiguity resting in the knowledge that God is at the controls. That's always the outlook of roller coaster fans.

I think there's a good chance there'll be roller coasters in heaven, and I can't wait. I want to ride in the front car, sitting next to my daddy again. When we disembark, I want to squeeze his neck and thank him again for introducing me to roller coasters and to the Father from whom comes every good gift. . . .even roller coasters.

So put your hands up.

Let go. He's got you. And He will never let you go.

Know this and enjoy the ride.

*Chapter 10*

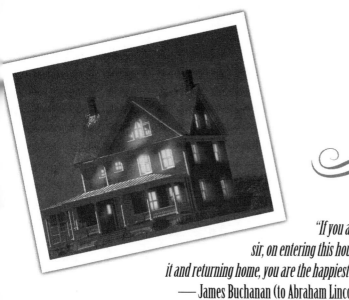

## Family Reunions

*"If you are as happy, my dear sir, on entering this house as I am in leaving it and returning home, you are the happiest man in the country."*
— James Buchanan (to Abraham Lincoln) [emphasis mine]

Every year we have a family reunion. That's been the case ever since I've been old enough to remember. Not many people know the Sigler site, a small patch by the Current River, in the depths of Southern Missouri, at Alley Springs park. Some years we're even lucky enough to get the shaded pavilion.

Some things are always the same. Too much food. Cheeks pinched by well-meaning elderly aunts. Grades, gymnastics, singing and basketball activities inquired about. Laps to sit on. Advice given. News to report on. Babies to pass around. Engagement rings to display. Wedding, graduation and vacation photos to share. Lots of loud, rowdy play with more cousins than there are kids in your entire elementary class.

Sticky fingers, dripping with watermelon juice. Flies. Midwestern June heat. Laughter. Uncle Jim's repetitive list of seemingly endless poor jokes.

"Whadya call a cow with no legs?"

"Ground beef!"

"Whadya call a cow with two legs?"

"Lean beef!"

"Got a new one this year, it's a real knee slapper! What's the difference between broccoli and boogers?"

Aunt Alice chimes in. "Jim, hush, we don't talk like that around the food!" Everyone knows he's going to finish anyway.

"Kids won't eat broccoli! Ha, ha, ha. . . .get it?"

A glare from Aunt Alice and he's back to the cow jokes.

"Whadya call a cow that's just had a calf?"

"Decaffeinated!"

Then someone, usually my dignified, well-read, but secretly ornery, Uncle Keith, gets everyone to hush, gather around and prepare to pray and bless the food. He usually called on my daddy.

In my mind's eye I can still see all of us, frozen like one of those black and white stills in a history photographer's coffee table picture book. Heads bowed. Pony-tailed heads. Gray, grizzled heads. Smooth, sleek heads. Flat tops. Eyes closed (mostly). Babies squirming in tanned arms. Someone slapping away a mosquito, feeding greedily on an unsuspecting ankle.

Without fail, I was always the one peeking, watching my daddy pray and offer thanks that family was together again. Trying to spot the secret pasts of those I'd overheard my parents whisper about. Meeting the eye of Uncle Hube, who'd look momentarily stern, and then wink. Marveling at Aunt Nancy's perpetual youth. Longing for another of aunt Margaret's wild stories. Wondering if I'd ever have someone special to bring to this ragtag group, joined by blood, marriage, shared history and a thousand separate experiences.

And then the Amen was spoken and the spell broken for another year.

After lunch, the kids all go down to swim in the river, the country folks scoffing at us tenderfeet from the cities. Who knew the rocks from a riverbed could hurt so much every year?

Some years, someone brings a fiancee, and so that poor, hapless soul must jump from Float Rock into the river, passing a symbolic rite of passage into the Sigler Clan. [If anyone's marriage ever falters, Uncle Keith is quick to point out that union must have skipped this test!] And then we walk over winding trails to get to the Alley Spring Mill. An old water wheel still churns an icy freshwater spring.

As a child daddy held us by our ankles so we could lean waaaay over and drink the water. Water so cold it made our teeth ache, and then pull up watercress for nibbling. Only last year I did the same for my girls.

But perhaps the best part are the stories. Bands of lawn chairs and overturned Styrofoam coolers circled into intimate groups, sharing tales, old and new.

The old story that we could never get enough of as kids and were repelled by as adults, about a great great grandfather who murdered his wife and then killed himself on the Fourth of July because he thought she was going to cheat on him. Hit the front page of the town's only newspaper and was quite possibly the last crime committed in Texas County (a dubious honor we're never sure whether to claim or disdain).

We begged to hear daddy, Uncle Keith and Uncle Hubert tell again and again about growing up in that house and looking for bloodstains on the wood floors. We tried hard to picture them as little boys fascinated by the macabre.

We couldn't get enough of my grandpa's exploits at the rodeo. Of my own parents' rocky courtship. The tornado that blew apart a home along with a great deal of memories. The well they had to draw water from as children. By the end of that story, our arms were just as tired and we could fairly feel the water that must have splashed against their calves as they lumbered the half mile home.

Stories of my grandmother's car wreck on her way to pick strawberries for my parents' wedding reception. Stories of her faith back before grandpa became so ill that she bought a dress for his funeral, but then God surprised everyone by granting him a miracle, and he spent the rest of his life preaching and building little country churches all over that area.

Stories of my daddy's basketball playing prowess and the merciless teasing he suffered at his brothers' hands and then promptly passed that on to his two little sisters.

Stories of my wonderful aunt who was Mayor of one of those small towns of my heritage. That same quirky, adventurous Aunt Margaret who bought and managed the same old-fashioned clothing store in Willow Springs that my grandmother shopped at during the 30s and 40s. It still had some of those World War II-era signs and the old glass counter holding ladies gloves and undergarments, and a selection of men's hats. How I loved the history, the feeling of pride and belonging in that musty place of memories old and new.

Family reunions always accomplished such things whether I knew it or not. It was a warm, imperfect, but accepting circle of my life. I was watched, scolded, mentored, cared for, loved. And I learned to hunger for a good story.

Of course there are always those relatives we feel stuck with, rather than proud of. Aunt Jane, who both dresses and acts like an ill-mannered bag lady, despite everyone's urges contrary. Uncle Timothy who's been in the pokey for some crime he committed, but nobody exactly talks about when or where. Uncle Jack, who's bad breath compels everyone to avoid him, trying to escape his annual boisterous peck on the forehead.

Uncle Dave, who's just a little too into philosophy and bores anyone he can pigeon hole and who's still breathing with his latest dull discoveries. Closet relatives, skeletons stacked high.

Some of those people, both beloved and flawed, are hard to live with. Nevertheless, we knew they were members of our extended family and we learned to love them anyway. A family reunion included them all.

The same is true of our church family. There are those who irritate us, who get on our nerves. Those who sing too loudly and off pitch. Those who give the longest, most boring communion meditations in the history of the Church. Those who seem too needy. Not with it. But we'd better practice. They will be living with us forever.

Each of us has smaller, miniature versions of reunions nearly every day. A quick phonecall, a group e-mail, a whirlwind visit to town. Campouts on the living room floor. A husband comes home from work. A child gets off the school bus. Family reunions, all. Small chances to celebrate, to love, to welcome.

The very way that we treat those in our earthly families and the family of God offer chances to practice for heaven's reunion. The late Mother Teresa, who gave her life to serve among the world's poorest in Calcutta, India, gracefully reminded us how the Christian life is to be lived.

People are often unreasonable, illogical, and self-centered;
Forgive them anyway.

If you are kind, people may accuse you of selfish, ulterior motives;
Be kind anyway.

If you are successful, you will win some false friends and some true enemies;
Succeed anyway.

If you are honest and frank, people may cheat you;
Be honest and frank anyway.

What you spend years building, someone could destroy overnight.
Build anyway.

If you find serenity and happiness, they may be jealous.
Be happy anyway.

The good you do today, people will often forget tomorrow.
Do good anyway.

Give the world the best you have, and it may never be enough;
Give the world the best you've got anyway.

You see, in the final analysis, it is between you and God;
It was never between you and them anyway.

~ Mother Teresa

How much we can learn when the body of believers becomes our family! How many occasions there are to mourn with each other, to comfort each other, to support each other, to celebrate someone's joy!

Like my friends, the Gardners, who married and for eight long years prayed for a child. The doctors assured them that one would not be forthcoming. But their daughter Joanna did arrive! And after being told that that birth was a fantastic miracle, the doctors were stunned when seven years after that, they became pregnant yet again. With twins! Both family and church family rejoiced.

Bible stories we've longed to know the rest of, characters in God's greatest drama that we've longed to meet with will unfold before us at a soon-to-be meeting of family. Rahab(I've always thought of her like sort of a Biblical Rapunzel, only with Longaberger baskets and ropes instead of long hair!); Moses, I wonder how many fish his bare feet had to step on during the crossing of the Red Sea; Zacchaeus - how short was he really? Does he smile when he hears my youngest daughter, Ellie, sing the chorus that tells his story over and over? Peter - who was his mother-in-law anyway? What about the night Paul escaped the city gate's by night, like a first century James Bond?

Just like the stories told on the banks of the Current River every June, we will have another family reunion. Oh the tales we shall hear and share.

Imagine it with me for a moment. You and I will both be attending together. Only you won't have to bring a bucket of fried chicken or attempt to keep a jello salad both cold and intact over curving roads in July heat. It's catered. The feast will be endless, calorie-free and more delicious than anything you've ever had. The beautifully laid table will extend boundless into the expanse of the universe.

Daughters will again greet daddies who've been absent from home for a while. Sons will hold tightly to the hands of those loved ones they haven't held for a while. Mothers will be reunited with children with whom they've had a wrenching parting and with tiny babies who didn't make it this side of heaven.

Husbands and wives who've weathered a lifetime of illness, struggles and hard work will meet again with eternal youth and lasting energy. Perhaps that fourth finger of their left hand will still bear a worn place to remind them of commitments kept. Brothers and sisters will clasp each other tightly. Unspeakable joy

War veterans and underground heroes who've died for freedom's cause will finally receive a fitting and proper decoration. Those we've admired and longed for will be met. The toils, sighs and sorrows of this journey will be over and we will experience reunion with all the Saints.

I will finally get to meet baby Elayna and hold for the first time, the children I never got to bring home from the hospital.

I will carry on my first conversation with my grandmother and thank her for her faith. I will be reunited with my beloved daddy and have forever to fill him in on all that he's missed.

What a scene! Shouting, praising, swapping stories and playing Twenty Questions with the Apostle Paul. We will together meet the One whose nail-scarred hands bought us admission to this most glorious of all reunions. And then, we will turn and throw ourselves at the feet of the Most High God, the eternal host and orchestrator of the best and final family reunion.

Chapter 11

*Popcorn &*
*Fireplaces*

*"I am beginning to learn that*
*it is the sweet, simple things*
*of life which are the real ones after all."*
— Laura Ingalls Wilder

*I* made a trip to the post office this morning and filled out a customs declaration form:

-purple rubber snake with fluorescent orange dots (for my nephew)
-Disney Winnie-the-Pooh stickers (for my niece)
- Christmas stationery
-a box of gourmet jelly bellies (including popcorn flavored ones)
-a handful of family photos

It doesn't seem like much unless you're my sister and her family, far away in Taiwan, working as missionaries, and watching for signs of home.

In my office, taped to my computer are six gel-penned Post-It notes, lovingly placed there by my oldest daughter, Eden. She wanted to be sure I could see them while I wrote. *Remember, I'm praying for you.* A list, printed in purple ink: *Brainstorm, write, beat deadline, imagine, research, read, think. You can meet your deadline. Say that over and over. God is with you always.* Brightly colored bits of encouragement. Simple, but treasured.

Often it's not the profound sentiment, the spectacular vacation or the expensive gift that makes the most lasting memories. It's the simple things.

The warm, melted marshmallow mustache you get from drinking cocoa. The way a newly sharpened pencil writes on ruled paper. Falling asleep holding your mate's hand. Burrowing under lots of quilts and napping on a rainy afternoon.

Sifting through old photo albums and scrapbooks. The first snow fall. Memory-making tickle fests with my girls. Caroling at Christmas. The crisp feel of brand new book cover. The dog-eared familiarity of a favorite book. Munching on popcorn popped on the stove the old-fashioned way, smothered in real melted butter and liberally sprinkled with salt.

Hayrides. Bonfires. Catching snowflakes on your tongue. Unexpected visits from old friends. The season's first fire in the fireplace. . . .and the last.

When I was in high school, I spent many Thursday nights in front of the fireplace, sitting up with my daddy, drinking icy Dr. Peppers and eating popcorn, watching Johnny Carson and discussing the things of life. (My mother goes to bed at 9:30 p.m. promptly. Has since I've known her, and would, even if the Queen of England came to visit!) Depending on the latest craze, we switched from buttery popped corn, to the more health-conscious air-popped corn, to microwave popcorn and back again.

But the topics never veered far from the basic stuff of life. An upcoming history test. My ogre math teacher. Why God intended intimacy to be reserved for marriage. The story of how he met and married my mother. The kind of man he and mother prayed that I would marry. Whether or not I could borrow the car that weekend. God's faithfulness. How proud he was of us girls. The topic of his upcoming sermon series. The encouragement of my life's dreams and goals.

I've forgotten the particular angst of the high school girl who poured out girlish woes to her father. Only two specific things stand out these many years later. That he truly believed I could accomplish anything, and that he was certain no plan succeeded without God's hand.

My husband is in charge of popping the corn at our house now. Every Sunday night is family night. Usually we can be found, camped out in the family room, sharing bowls of popcorn and watching *The Waltons, Andy Griffith or Little House On The Prairie.* The spirit of Walton's Mountain, Mayberry and Walnut Grove seem a perfect antedote to today's faster-paced living.

We discuss the lessons of getting along with family and the history incorporated into those shows. We read books aloud and often we have devotions together. Sometimes we have a family meeting. Many times we pray.

We pray for new puppies, new babies, angels, spelling tests and friends who've hurt us. We share with our girls the simplicity of the Gift God shared with us and the nutshell of what He requires of us. "To act justly and to love mercy and to walk humbly with your God." (Micah 6:8)

We are keenly aware that the time given to us to pass the baton of faith and the heritage of heaven on to our girls is all too short. Sometimes we drop that baton. We react instead of acting. We get grouchy. We have less faith than we'd like to. We worry sometimes. But we try to model how to meet those problems on our knees. We want our girls to hunger for God and popcorn and fireplaces. To strive for integrity, for purity, for faithfulness.

Like the story of Hansel & Gretl, we are dropping crumbs that they may find their way Home. Only instead of vanishing, windblown bread crumbs dropped from a pocket, they are crumbs from the Bread of Life. God assures us that will be enough.

Remember where the path leads? It leads us back Home.

The saying goes, "Change is like heaven, everyone likes the concept, but nobody wants to start the process." We laugh, but when is the last time you wanted to go Home? *Really* wanted to go to heaven?

When Eden was three, she helped me hang some Easter vinyl clings on our dining room window. There was one of three crosses, one of an empty tomb and one of Jesus, ascending into heaven. I pointed to each one, asking her to explain their significance and beaming with pride as she told me.

Then I asked her if she knew how you got to heaven. Confidently she replied, "Well, you have to be old or sick or dead first!" Hmmm. . . doesn't sound very appealing does it?

It's not easy getting to heaven. Our hearts groan with longing because we are not at home. But God is good enough to send us timeless moments that "send our hearts on ahead to heaven", as Joni Eareckson Tada writes in her book, *Heaven Our Real Home.*

Part of the reason her writing is so inspirational is because of her extraordinary courage in the face of quadriplegic paralysis. She brings success in that struggle to all of us. "Yours may not be physical (like mine)" she said when I heard her speak at the 1992 North American Christian Convention in Anaheim, California, "instead you may be paralyzed by a broken heart, a broken home, a broken reputation, but heaven offers hope."

If you remember reading or performing the play, *Our Town,* in high school, you'll recall that Emily dies, but is allowed to observe her family and friends on earth. She is keenly aware of all that she took for granted. She remembers the little pleasures like "sunflowers, coffee, new-ironed dresses and hot baths." She asks the stage manager, "Do human beings ever realize life while they live it? Every, every minute?"

Sadly, the answer is that most of us do not. We forget to revel in popcorn and fireplaces. We forget how much of the simplicity of life is a shell of eternal moments. We forget to be caught up in the sheer joy of living.

Molly, our golden retriever, on these golden sunny days, brilliant with color and cozily lazy with the promise of winter ahead, wriggles around in the grass on her back, snorting and sighing with sheer pleasure. Almost, I am tempted to join her.

Pieces of heaven on earth are like that.

Heaven is when we choose to do what's right when it's hard.

When we're hospitable to those whom we wouldn't ordinarily seek out.

When we ignore the chores and play just one more game of Hi Ho Cherry O or build just one more block tower.

Pieces of heaven rain down when we *really* listen.

I seem a little more restless lately. In fact the whole world seems a little more restless. And I think it's because we're watching for signs of Home.

Pieces of heaven are really like bits of stardust, lining the path toward Home. Sprinkle them every chance you get and you may find that Home is closer than you think. Don't you want to go Home?

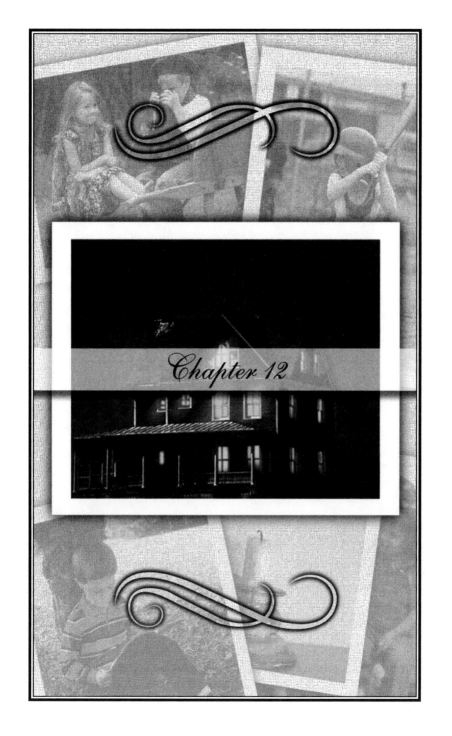

Chapter 12

## Under the Maples

*"There are only two ways to live your life. One is as though nothing is a miracle. The other is as though everything is a miracle."*
— Albert Einstein

*I* was out of the porch swing and down the steps in two giant motions. My three year old, Emmy, was howling and sobbing, and my eight year old, Eden, and her little neighbor friends were attempting to cower nonchalantly under the wooden fort near the row of sheltering maple trees.

In a TERRIBLE voice (in the *Wizard of Oz/Chronicles of Narnia* sense) I asked, "Girls, what happened?! Tell me this minute!"

Emmy pointed to her head where a red knot was starting to emerge. I knelt to assure myself that she was okay, and then fixed a steely gaze on the other children. Eden was quick to explain. Holding up a still-green walnut, she offered, "One of these hit her in the head?"

"How?"

"Well," she looked at her feet and shifted. "We were throwing them at each other because we were playing tornado and this is supposed to be the stuff that flies around in one."

I stared at her in amazement and choked, "I see. Well at any rate, we don't throw walnuts at people. Especially not little sisters!"

Then I turned and fled to the shelter of the porch so she

would not see my unexpected laughter at their unwitting cruelty.

Ah, if only trees could talk. I'm sure they'd have stories to tell. Tales of daring played out under their branches. Cops and robbers. Tag. Tea Parties. Hide & seek. Of confidences exchanged under their boughs. Of simple shelter sought there.

Trees whose trunks have been carved with the initials of first love. Branches who've been whittled into charming carvings or pressed into service for bonfires or marshmallow roasts.

Trees who've received the honor of gracing a family room at Christmastide, branches laden with glass balls, hand-carved creches, strings of popcorn and cranberries and shimmery spheres made of tin foil, paste and glitter.

Trees who've been chopped into cords of firewood. Sawed into planks of lumber for desks, chairs, bed frames, floors and homes. Trees that have served as harbingers of death in old-time executions. Trees that shelter life in their branches. The electric blue of robin eggs in the spring. Squirrel nests. The tangy sweetness of oranges. The crisp crunch of apples. Squealing children on tire swings and in tree houses, their scraped and gangly limbs dangling precariously opossum-like from lower boughs.

There are two trees in our yard that I like. Lots. The tallest, most colorful maple in the windbreak at the east side of our home. It's the one where I like to sit and write, dream, think. And a majestic pine tree, directly in front of the house. It was planted there in the sixth grade by one of the former occupants of this house. Each time I look at it, I am reminded of the fleeting passage of time and the importance of making memories. The little girl who planted that tree is all grown-up now, with children of her own. She lives next door.

I remember all of this as I watch my girls play under the

trees, swing from their branches and climb their heights. I engrave all of these memories in my mind, capture them in movies and paste them into scrapbooks.

Engravings. We have them done on picture frames, Bible covers and photo albums. We engrave things because we want them to last.

Carvings. I was once in a relationship where someone who promised me his undying love carved a message for me on a park bench. For a while, we both checked on the message and rejoiced when it was still there. Then rain, snow, the passage of time, a new coat of paint and other carvings took its place. But it was probably just as well. He didn't keep his promises.

Telling tales. Yes, trees could tell tales. Loves won and lost. Worlds conquered and retaken. Markings that whisper of gentle rains, cuts that shout of storms weathered and blows withstood.

A few weeks ago, I told my husband that I thought it would be hopelessly romantic if he would carve our initials into the trunk of that favorite maple tree. *It'd be hopeless, all right,* he muttered.

But whether he ever carves the message of our love on that tree or not, I know of another tree where someone already has carved a message of eternal love for me. The cross.

The most important engraving ever took place on that tree. The old rugged cross imprinted us on the face of God's heart and on the nail-scarred hands of His Son.

*"I will not forget you. See, I have inscribed you on the palms of my hands."*

-Isaiah 49:15-16 NRSV

It is *this* tree that reminds me of two things: the astounding depth of God's love for me and of what's real and what really matters in this life. . . .

When we were first married, my husband worked the three to midnight shift back in detectives. Sometimes he'd get home late and get called right back out. Made me exhausted! I'd lie awake, missing him and worrying. (Must've worked too. 95% of what I worried about never happened). After a few months, he bought me a teddy bear. I named it Muffin. "Whenever I get called out," my husband instructed, "go get Muffin and cuddle with him until I get home." I love Muffin, but he's not my *real* husband. **There is no substitute for the real thing.**

I have a tendency to get caught up in the pretty, but shallow baubles of this world too. And then I remember, *I can love this world, and all of the good things God has placed here for our enjoyment. . . . but, it's not my real home.* **Earth is but a prelude to the real thing.**

I could have met some deadlines this morning, but I chose instead to take a walk with my girls. It took us twenty minutes to go fifteen feet. My oldest daughter, Eden, rode her bicycle around us in circles, prodding us to *"Come on!"* with the striking impatience of youth. But Emily and baby Ellie were not to be hurried. We stooped to feel the fuzzy backs of each caterpillar. We admired a walking stick and shoved our fingers into the prickly openings of a pinecone. We stopped to pick a few straggling wildflowers, shoot a basket at the end of the lane, and pat the cows on their noses through the fence. We waved maniacally to the mailman and examined the rippled pattern on the blacktop.

When it was time to turn around and head for home, we sat down under the maples. Using acorn caps and fallen autumn leaves for cups and saucers, we drank some of the best imaginary tea I've ever tasted.

Trees have always been good for making memories. I remember trees tied with yellow ribbons and the breath of a song, *Tie a yellow ribbon 'round the old oak tree* . . . to express first hope, and then welcome to those who were away from home. Makes me wonder if there are any ribbons on trees in heaven.

We moved into this dilapidated farm house during the heat of summer. It seemed the only cool place was under the green lushness of those maple trees. Before it seemed possible, a brisk October wind ushered in the majesty of autumn. The maples caught fire - a blaze of orange, red and yellow.

Winter came and those trees waved their shadowy, skeletal branches like inky stick arms against a powdery white canvas. When I became so sick of hearing the eerie howl of blizzard winds through that row of trees I could've cheerfully chopped them down, tiny buds of spring green pushed the last of the snow off the branches in winter's promise, which is always spring.

While the trees marked time outside, I dipped each girl's hand in a pan of paint and stamped its imprint on the wall, along with a pencil carving of their heights and the date.

I wanted to preserve the memories before today went tumbling into next year.

Maybe that's why I love being under the maple trees so much. Because to me they symbolize the miracle of seasons, the miracle that is life, the miracle of grace.

Every night I tuck in three miracles: Eden Victoria, Emily Savannah and Elizabeth Grace. I am awestruck at these gifts. Soon I will tuck in a fourth.

Every morning I wake up to a miracle. A godly man who loves me against all reason. A soul mate with whom God has made me one.

It's nothing short of a miracle to live in a country of such progress, patriotic pride and the good sense to allow all of us the freedom of worship.

117

It's miraculous to have eyes that see, ears that hear, legs that run, lungs that breathe and an approaching mid-life body that can still touch my toes. Sort of.

It's a miracle that the air where I live is sultry and hazy on summer evenings and crisp and crackling clean on bright winter mornings.

The waves that crash endlessly against the ocean's shore In rapid succession and then retreat to the other side of the world, are miraculous.

But there are even better miracles. I serve a God who knows the number of hairs on my head and the number of stars in the sky.

I love a God who used every color in the BIG box of sixty-four Crayons when creating our world. A God who began His work with some trees in the Garden, fulfilled His work on a tree at Golgotha and completed His work with the Tree of Life. We'll see it as soon as we get Home.

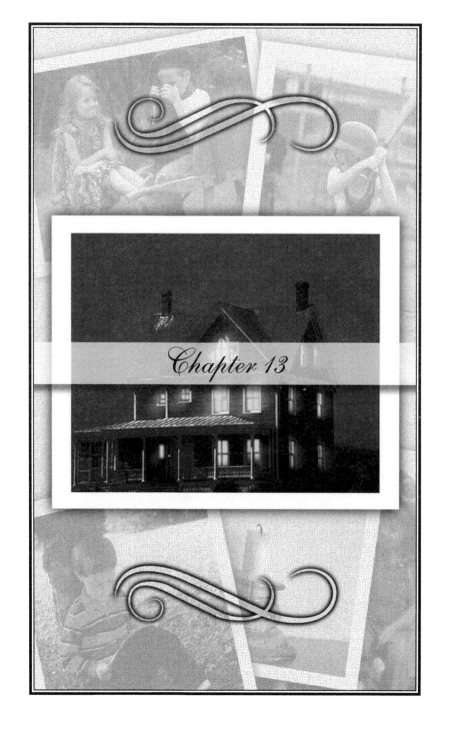

Chapter 13

*The Smells of*
*Home*

*"Nothing else smells like home."*
— Janine King

*I*f comfort had a smell, I think it would be home. If you could smell contentment, I imagine it'd smell like home.

Ever notice how each house has its own distinct smell? An eclectic mix that becomes a personality of sorts. Some are pleasant, some overpowering and others are, uh, unpleasant.

I love many of the smells that speak to me of home.

~ the smell of starch and water as it squirts from my mother's spray bottle on ironing day.

~ the warm, smell of sunshine wafting through damp clothes breezily waltzing on the clothesline.

~ just-mown grass.

~ the pungent smell of damp earth and concrete sidewalks after a warm spring rain.

~ the soapy summertime smell of a huge bucket filled with Palmolive and warm water on car washing day.

If you turned the key and walked inside my childhood home, a different cacophony of scents assailed your nose. Lemon paste wax, vanilla and the woodsy, smoke smell of the fireplace. Perhaps the delicate sweet fragrance of just picked roses from the bushes in the backyard. The familiar dinner smells of roasting meat and onion.

Mother could most often be found cooking in the kitchen or curled up on a corner of the sofa, reading. When I was a little girl, she wore the perfume *White Shoulders*. To this day, I associate it with comfort, a warm lap and exceptional acceptance. For the lady who smelled of it, admired my drawings, kept my confidences and actually wore some of the outlandish Mother's Day gifts I made for her.

Downstairs was the laundry room and daddy's office. My sister, Angie, and I often peeked through the vent in the laundry room, watching daddy work. The hum of the washing machine and the warm pleasant scent of detergent and clothes slapping against the drum of the dryer accompanied our spy sessions. We watched daddy type, study, pray and rehearse his sermons. Sometimes, he would catch us, but pretending not to see us, he would point a finger at our little white puppy, and say, "Marshmellow! Repent!" We would collapse in laughter and burst into the study, which smelled of daddy's aftershave and old bottles of correction fluid. What a welcoming combination to two bored little girls on rainy afternoons!

The smells of home.

Certain smells transport me to other places, other times or specific events. The combination of hot, buttered popcorn, roasting hot dogs, dusty peanut shells, sticky sweet carbonation and packed earth takes me back to Busch Stadium in my home town of St. Louis.

The clean, crisp, fresh smell of newly fallen snow takes me swooshing down a hill, piled on the sled with daddy and my sister. I can almost hear our whoops and squeals as the sled runners beat the snow into thin gray ropes and the crunch of our snow boots as we trudged uphill for still another ride.

Opening a jar of school paste, I am instantly back in Ms. George's third grade class room creating valentines with scraps of lace, doilies, crayons and construction paper.

Honeysuckle transports me to the fence in the backyard of my childhood home and the never-ending games of Annie Over and Hide & Seek there on lazy summer nights.

Leafing through the pages of an old journal and reading the descriptions I recorded there, I recall noticing on my trip to Europe that even *cities and countries* smell different! The bustling, big city smell of London, England, packed with the exhaust of checkered cabs and double decker tour busses. The indescribably rich smell of chocolatiers in Switzerland (man, can they make chocolate)! The intense fruit and leather smells of open air markets in Rome, Italy. The putrid smell of the stagnant water of the canals under St. Mark's Cathedral in Venice. The clear fresh scent of the Alps and apple strudel topped with beaten schlog (cream) in Austria. The musty dank smell of history in Munich, Germany.

Whether we've thought about it or not, fragrance fills our lives. And evidently our noses are sensitive things. Studies show that under normal conditions you can smell *one drop* of perfume diffused through a three room apartment!

Store retailers know the role that our senses, including smell, play in getting customers to consume. That's why they often light candles, set out bowls of potpourri and place the perfume and cologne counters near the front. Add a backdrop of soothing music and colorful displays, and well, most of us are goners!

If our senses are engaged, for better or worse, so are our memories (and yes, sometimes, our pocketbooks). Who can forget their first experience with "new car" smell, and the accompanying wish to drive it home? The thrill if you actually left the showroom with that car?

And I'm willing to bet that if someone blind-folded you and took you to a hospital or nursing home, you could recognize either place, just by their strong, peculiar odors.

Ever been reduced to rummaging for your apples in the produce section of a grocery store only to long for childhood outings to a local orchard? The kind where the sweet smell of pick-your-own apples and cider filled a musty barn?

Scents are locked in our memories and may be retrieved by the trigger of a familiar sight or smell. If I look at old pictures of my childhood home, I can smell it. My girls have an old scratch 'n' sniff Christmas book that belonged to me as a child. The scratch marks have long since obliterated the smells, but as I read the story to my girls, I can still remember the scent of each page: the candy cane, the gingerbread man, the steaming mug of cocoa, and the pine of the tree that the bear family hauled home for Christmas.

Whenever Eden, our oldest daughter, leaves home for a sleepover or a session of church camp, she always wants me to spray her teddy bear with my vanilla-caramel scented perfume. She tells me that when she smells it as she drifts off to sleep, she can pretend that she's at home. My husband, Greg, also requests that same perfume on our date nights, because it's the scent I wore on our wedding day.

Greg was a patrol officer and police detective for seven years and is now the investigator for the prosecuting attorney's office. He has many interesting stories about the smells he's encountered on the job. So strong is the association between memory and smell, that when he simply *looks* through a set of autopsy photographs, in preparation for a trial, he can literally *smell* the formaldehyde and embalming fluid. If you were to catalog all the scents of your experience, you'd be surprised at the memories a given smell brings to mind.

Perhaps the unforgettable smells of home are never quite as clear as at Christmas time. Fresh pine. Vanilla and the scent of warm sugar cookies. Cinnamon pinecones. Savory turkey. Sage stuffing. Hot wassail. Yeasty bread. Woodsmoke. Sweet raisins. Fragrant nut meats. Aunt Eileen's perfume, as she hugs you to her scratchy wool coat, still smelling of the wet snow, clinging to the collar. What the new puppy did in your laundry room where you're trying to hide him from the kids until Christmas morning. The pulpy smell of cardboard wrapping paper rolls. The precious talc and lotion baby smell of your newborn cradled in a blanket sleeper and Uncle Hank's arms. Ah, Christmas!

I wonder what it smelled like that first Christmas night. Probably not as sanitary as the manger scenes in our homes make it seem. Our family recently went to Branson, Missouri for the Radio City Music Hall Rockettes Christmas Extravaganza. (Whew!) The last scene was a live nativity. The entire re-enactment was spectacular and moving. But what struck me were the smells of the stable. Mary rode into Bethlehem on a donkey. *They don't smell pretty.* There were sheep and cows pawing through the hay in their stalls. Then the wisemen made their journey camelback, and well, I don't know how they removed the stench from their brocaded tunics before dry-cleaning was available!

God came to earth, born in a shelter meant to house animals, because He loved us. He worked hard and sometimes smelled of sweat. He took tax money from the mouths of fishes. He healed people who forgot to thank Him and preached to folks that were ungrateful. Then He died. He smelled of humanity and he smelled of hope. If that can't move us, we're out of hope.

I wonder what the Galilee of Jesus' day smelled of. Fresh fish lying in nets and baskets, waiting to be scaled and brought to the marketplace? Ripe with the strong odor of big, strapping fishermen who had worked all day? The smell of

125

wet sand? The dry, brushy smell of desert? The overpowering smell of camel fur?

I particularly wonder about one biblical smell. The smell of the perfume offered by the sinful woman (this is the only way the Bible identifies her). A "woman who had lived a sinful life in that town."{Luke 7:37, NIV} Apparently everyone in town knew her. No need to name names. The Amplified Bible calls her "an especially wicked sinner." She knew the power of scent. No doubt she had used its sensual benefits when plying her trade. But in this story, she transformed its power into a most unique offering to Jesus. She anointed Him with a jar of costly, aromatic perfume. Then more importantly, she anointed His feet with her tears and her submission. Surrender - a total sell-out to the Lord of her life.

That's what I want. A home whose aroma reflects the joy, the surrender, the love experienced by lives sold-out to God. A home where play and work, fellowship and fun dwell side by side.

The smell of the first chill, driving rain of fall wafted under the front door. Large drops drove under the wide white porch and pelted the rockers, porch swing and the whiskey barrel sporting checkers and a stenciled game board.

Two noses pressed wistfully against the glass. Then they turned and fixed their baleful gazes on me. My husband also looked at me with eyes full of questions. "How 'bout it, Cinso? Would it be okay if we went ahead with our basketball game anyway?"

I think I gave my husband the shock of his life. "Go ahead," I answered. "It won't kill the girls to get sopping wet for ten minutes. I'll have a hot bath and cocoa waiting."

I snapped and tied hoods and sent them off amidst raucous squealing. The baby and I watched through the screen door applauding any and all shots. The aroma of soggy earth and wet wood drifted in.

After a few minutes, one of the lawyers in the prosecutor's office where my husband is investigator, drove up the lane to deliver some papers for an upcoming trial. "Just in time for the game," my husband invited. He shook his head in refusal and stared at the lot of us like we were crazy. Maybe he wouldn't nominate me for mother of the year, but I'm sure my three and eight year old daughters thought I was in the running. As his car backed out of the driveway, I thought he might secretly be a little jealous. Maybe we're not crazy, we're just enjoying the smells of home.

*Crazy.* I shook my head. *We must have been crazy to say we'd teach tonight's Vacation Bible School lesson to all the age groups, including second graders!*

My husband was hiding out in a makeshift pup tent behind a staged campfire, whose flashlighted red tissue paper flames crackled convincingly thanks to a rattling fan. (I promise he wasn't actually avoiding the kids; it was part of the lesson).

As we heard the next group of children being herded toward the classroom door, I reached up my hands to knead my neck muscles and sighed at the seemingly hopeless task.

How to explain to this squirming, noisy mass of seven and eight year olds about feet. Beautiful feet that carry the Good News. About the importance of our footprints and where they go. About the Home that we will dwell in together.

I greeted my young charges and erstwhile students barefoot. I wriggled my painted red toes in front of them and then asked them to remove *their* shoes. *Whew! This is going to be more challenging than I thought.* Instead of holding my nose, I held my breath for a second and exhaled.

"I have beautiful feet, don't you think?" They giggled. "Now look at yours. You have beautiful feet too. Know how I know that? God says that we have beautiful feet if we share the Good News of His Son with others. Now I'd like to introduce you to my friend, Philip, a man with extraordinary feet."

I scurried to the light switch so they would be surprised when my husband Greg, aka Philip, crawled out of the tent and shared with them the story of his encounter with the Ethiopian eunuch.

As children do when presented with even a halfway convincing drama, they sat spellbound. When Greg finished we all talked about other things Philip could have done, instead of obeying God. We talked about the custom of foot washing in Jesus' day and the importance of making sure our footprints stayed on the right path. A path that would one day lead Home.

When the lights came back on, I discovered that during the story, the children had scooted up until they were nearly on top of our feet. I looked across the sea of eager, innocent faces and suddenly nothing had ever smelled sweeter than the nineteen pairs of beautiful, stinky feet on that VBS classroom floor.

It reminded me of another lesson about smells and feet. You can read it in John 13:1-17. Jesus, King of the heavens and the earth, assumes yet another position of servanthood. He stoops and washes the feet of His disciples. He ". . . took off his outer clothing, and wrapped a towel around his waist. After that, he poured water into a basin and began to wash his disciples' feet, drying them with the towel that was wrapped around him." {v. 4,5}

This isn't just a sweet story, make no mistake about it. It's a story about smells and a servant's heart. The disciples knew perfectly well that it was both custom and courtesy (a necessity, really) to wash the feet of guests after their long, dusty walks. The catch was, this supper wasn't in anyone of their homes. It took place in a prepared, upper guest room. We aren't told much more than that.

If we were privy to the disciples' thoughts, I wonder what they'd have been. *Glad this isn't my house! I mean, have you seen Peter's feet? They're big and hairy and man do they smell bad! John has gritty stuff stuck between his toes. I can see it - ugh! Thomas' sandals are so old they positively reek! i told him he should've had some new ones made at the cobbler's place in Capernaum. They got soaked last time we were out on the boat. Maybe everybody'll forget and we can just skip the whole thing this one time . . .*

Certainly, nobody was thinking about the weary, soon-to-be-pierced feet of the Savior. But He was sure thinking about them. He must've been tired. The crowds hadn't quit badgering Him since the Triumphal Entry. And the Pharisees were furious. *See, this is getting us nowhere. Look how the whole world has gone after him!* {John 12:19} And yet Jesus knew that shortly one of His own would betray Him and the whole world would turn against Him.

He assumes the posture of a servant and dips a cloth into the water in the basin. He starts at one end of the table and moves from disciple to disciple. Cleansing. Running the cloth between filthy toes. Moving gently over calluses. Massaging tough insteps. It's interesting that scripture doesn't record anyone jumping up to return the favor. Or even that Jesus washed His own feet. When He's finished, He sits back on His heels and gently admonishes: *"Now that I, your Lord and Teacher, have washed your feet, you also should wash one another's feet. I have set you an example that you should do as I have done for you."* (John 13:14,15)

And what an example! God washing dirty feet. I'll have to remember that the next time I want to nag my children about a forgotten chore. The next time I'm tempted to roll my eyes at the juvenile antics of an irritating acquaintance. The next time I plot to leave something undone because my mate said he'd take care of it. (Afterall, if I outwait him, I can read a few more chapters in my book; watch a few more minutes of my show; stay a little longer under the shower spray). The next time I decide that my needs are most important. Maybe if we all engaged in a little more foot washing, the smells of home would be sweeter.

> *"For we are to God the aroma of Christ among those who are being saved and those who are perishing. To the one we are the smell of death; to the other, the fragrance of life. . ."*
>
> *-II Corinthians 2:15,16*

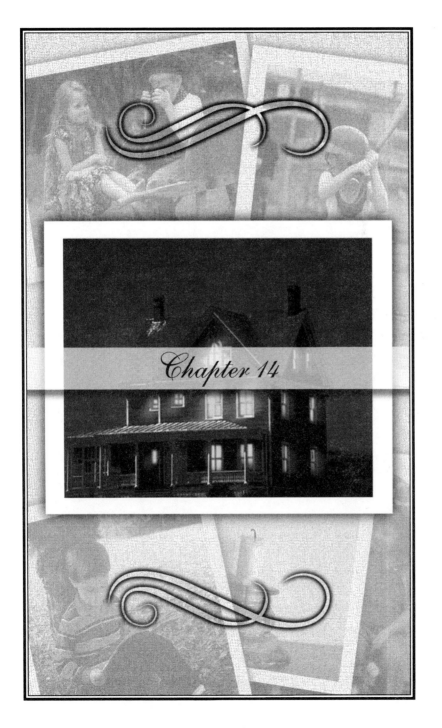

Chapter 14

# Frogs and Fireflies

*"Go out into the darkness and put your hand into the Hand of God. That shall be to you better than light and safer than a known way."*
— Minnie Louise Haskins

On the summer nights of my childhood, there was nothing I wanted so much as a pet firefly. My sister and I collected hundreds of them in washed out baby food and Mason jars, We stocked the jar bottoms with pieces of grass and interesting looking twigs. Then we lovingly punched holes in the jar lids so our festive captives could breathe. Taking them to our bedrooms, we thought how wonderful it would be to have our sleep hours illuminated by their softly blinking lights. Alas, within a few minutes the illusive glow always died.

God's creatures have often taught me valuable lessons. Lessons about God's infinite wisdom, limitless patience and awesome power. Beyond that which we ask or imagine. Afterall, can one presume to limit God? For how can one box in the God of the platypus? The God of the hyena's contagious laugh? The God of thunderstorms, tiny babies, sunflowers, glaciers, fireflies, and yes, even frogs? You can't. His power is manifest in the miracle of creation and in the dailyness of life.

A cool cloudy day in mid-September, sometimes in the late-nineteen seventies. The day looked as though it might escape rain, but in the early afternoon, an autumn drizzle pasted the blades of freshly mown grass to the black-topped driveway. It was funeral day and I must have been all of eleven years old.

Dad, in his large navy blue overcoat, held a black Mary Poppins umbrella over the heads of my five year old sister and me. Our destination was the backyard funeral service for two goldfish and one dehydrated gerbil, whom my sister had forgotten to water.

Our saddle oxfords sunk in the spongy earth as our pets, encased in our parents' red and black checkbook box coffins, were lowered into their graves. My father prayed and we sand a hymn. Our childish hearts fervently wished Sunshine, Shadow and Fluffy (who was now very flat) into"Animal Heaven."

That was the first time that I had ever grasped that things could die, even those things which were close and valuable to me. But in my dad, I saw the compassion of our heavenly Father as he knelt with a garden spade (having sacrificed his checkbook boxes) and tenderly buried those creatures outside in the rain. He won great respect in the eyes of two little girls who held hands with each other and with the strong, encompassing ones of both her fathers.

After the glamour of my senior prom, ny date and I arrived home rather wilted. We stood on the porch for a while basking in the afterglow of the fun, the memories and the thrill of being seniors. At a very pivotal moment, a frog jumped directly between my red satin pumps. End of romance. End of evening.

Apparently, Raincloud is not a very good name for a kitten. When the nice couple from church offered us a kitten to cut on the mice (we were remodeling a ninety-five year old farmhouse) it seemed like a great idea. Raincloud moved to our home on Buttercup Farm three days before Thanksgiving. Upon our return from an our-of-town Thanksgiving celebration, Raincloud was nowhere to be found. Obviously she had found our distinct lack of hospitality not worth staying around for. The children were sad.

Fortunately (depending on one's perspective) a few weeks later, the news of our loss got around, and we were offered a new tiny gray kitten by a kind neighbor down the road. It's name? Raincloud II. Raincloud lived as a member of the Dagnan household for three days. On his last day with us, Raincloud inadvertently took a ride in the wheel well of our minivan all the way to Walmart. He did not survive the trip. A wooden cross, colored with indelible markers, marks the spot where Raincloud II now rests. The children were devastated. Life is too fleeting, they decided. No more kittens.

But hope spring sternal and all that, so a month later, Snowball and Josephine came to live with us. They seemed to understand the job description — barn cats. We figure that the name change and safety in numbers did the trick. Three months later, they're still hanging around.

We've all had days just like the animals in those stories. We long for something we think will bring us happiness, but the glow is quickly extinguished.

Or we lose someone so dear to us that the knowledge we won't see them again this side of heaven seems more than we can bear.

We're beset by a chronic illness that saps our strength and steals our hope.

We think we're about to discover Prince Charming and then the frog lands smacks on our feet.

Life is giving us a raw deal, we think, so we just turn tail and run. We desert friendships, obligations, responsibilities.

Or worse yet, the daily wear and tear of the ordinary slowly kills us. Like Raincloud II, we've been spun around the wheel well too many times. We are knocked around, bruised and disillusioned. We feel flat like the deceased goldfish and out of refreshment like Fluffy.

Have you been there? Good news, Jesus was too.

Playing amid the wood shavings of the carpenter's bench in Nazareth, Jesus knew happiness. No doubt he played with the other boys. Tag, perhaps. A primitive for of stick hockey with the scrap lumber. Hide and seek. Pharisees versus Sadducees. As carefree as God as a young boy could be. But then He had to grow up in a hurry. He was teaching at the temple at the age of twelve and already feeling the weight of His heavenly responsibilities.

Immediately following his baptism, Satan was after Him. *"Go for the firefly pleasures, Jesus. Bow to me and all the kingdoms of the world are yours."* Jesus resisted, knowing that such things are temporary, at best. But He was dog-tired and ravenous. Life on earth was tough.

He stayed busy helping the caterers at friend's wedding reception and feeding thousands at impromptu picnic that had gotten out of hand.

When his good friend Lazarus died, Jesus wept. On the cross he cried out to His Father and Maker of the tree he was nailed to, "*My God, my God, why has thou forsaken me?*" Yes. He knew the pain of death and the utter misery of abandonment.

One week the crowds are frantically waving palm branches and cheering, "Hosanna! Hosanna!" Not a month later they were yelling ugly curses. "Crucify Him! Crucify Him!" He was betrayed by Judas and then Peter. Not mere acquaintances, these men, but his friends. His disciples, with whom he had shared the intimacy of miles, dreams and prayers.

Pharisees tried to trap him. The Jews called him a blasphemer. Crowds alternately adored and deserted him. People wanted him. His time, his healing, his compassion, his answers. Wanted what they thought he would do for them instead of what he really *could* do for them.

Jesus experienced all of life, just as we do. Jesus' feet got dirty. He got tired. Tired of crowds, tired of obligations. He was homesick. He missed his Father. He has felt wrung out and done in.

He ate. He drank. He talked. He went to parties. He walked. He preached. He taught. He healed. He put up with dumb questions and even dumber answers (think the rich young ruler, Nicodemus and the argument with James and John over who got to sit where)

His best friend, John the Baptist, was beheaded on the same day a violent storm shook up the sea of Galilee, and not incidentally, the faith of his followers.

He has walked on water, in fire, through doors and out of tombs. But He has also walked into the future. And it is safe to walk into the future holding the hand of the One who has been there.

He was there when the frog received his croaking voice and funny legs. He helped place the yellow lights in the tails of fire flies. He flung out his hands and coated the leopard with spots. He threw back his head and laughed with the hyena.

He knew at the moment of creation that we would sin; that some would scoff at His gift, but He came to earth anyway.

There is nothing you can't tell Him and nothing He won't understand. He knows how it feels to have a dream die. What happens when the charming becomes froglike. He remembers the gossamer brush of the firefly's wing and the appeal of its tiny light. He knows how fragile are our wishes;how real our hopes and disappointments.

And oh, how He loves you.

I learned fro those late night fire fly expedition that all good things must come to an end. But when life seems as futile as chasing fireflies, hang on the momentary glow in the Mason jar. 'Cause someday it will last forever.

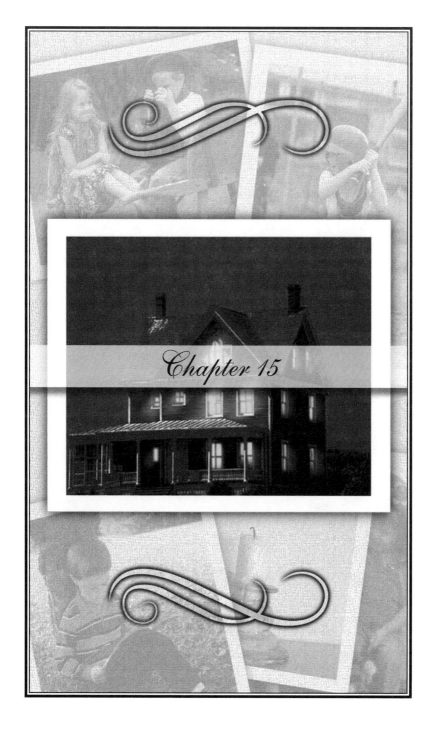

Chapter 15

# Sunday Dinner

*"What one loves in childhood stays in the heart forever."*
— Mary Jo Putney

*I* grew up thinking that roast, carrots and potatoes came out of the oven all by themselves after church.

Now I know better, for it's my turn, and in retrospect, I salute my mother and mothers everywhere. It's much harder work than I thought as a child. I set the alarm, get up earlier than my family and start Sunday dinner. Flouring and browning the roast, scraping carrots, peeling potatoes, slicing onions, punching down bread dough.

Sleepy, tousled heads are gently awakened by the sounds, smells and anticipation of dinner. I help three little girls choose their "Sunday Best" for God, just as my mother did for us long ago. Then we go downstairs for breakfast and pick out some "Sunday Morning Music" to prepare our hearts for worship.

And on some mornings, as I follow my babies downstairs, I can hear the echo of that long ago Sunday Morning Music at my childhood home. In a little while, we will head out the door for the Lord's house. But for now I savor the moment. And I think ahead to the Ultimate Sunday Dinner that awaits all of us and the eternal feast that will follow.

Luke 14:15-24 records an invitation to a feast. The nicest, richest, most compassionate, wonderful man on the block wants us to attend his party! Think of it! In this sacred romance, we are the fulfillment of His desire, just as He is ours. How awesome this love, how magical the dinner invitation!

Where did we get the idea that Christian living is miserable? Dour. Pious. Aloof. Barren. Not from God, that's for sure.

This will be a feast of abundance, a smorgasbord of delectable choices. Can't you envision the very best food of all the world gathered together, cooked to perfection in one place? Shrimp cocktail. A cheeseball molded in the shape of the pearly gates and crackers, cut out like the Book of Life. Chicken enchiladas. Crispy egg rolls. Heaping bowls of seasoned rice. Steamy platters of fresh corn. Succulent steaks. Fragrant carved roast beef. An omelet station. Pancakes and Belgian waffles. Spicy sausages. Chocolate layer cakes. Caramel apple pies. Icy pitchers of raspberry tea. Warm truffle coffee. Crystal clear water. And the Bread of Life. The Water that will never leave us thirsty.

There's just something intimate and celebrative about sharing a meal together. Meals are sustenance providing, but they are also soul nourishing. Seems like some of the best conversations, the funniest stories are exchanged around the table.

It's why second grade Thanksgiving plays include scenes of Pilgrims and Indians feasting on turkey and corn. It's why we're constantly asking folks over for pie and coffee, Sunday roast or homemade ice-cream and lemonade. Food is a reason to fellowship.

It's why we choose restaurants or special home-cooked dinners to celebrate birthdays, engagements, births, anniversaries. Food and fellowship, and sometimes even miracles, go together.

The book of Acts also invites us to look in on a community

who broke bread together. . . Mary and Martha shared Sabbath dinners with the Lord. So did a boy who had a simple sack lunch of five loaves and two fish. Jesus had lunch with sinners and partied with the tax collectors. He knew the value of sharing with people in such a common, necessary daily ritual. He did it for love. He did it because He knows how important it is for us to give.

The fine, lost art of hospitality. We've forgotten that meals prepared and shared with others are labors of love. It doesn't really matter if it's a four course dinner or carry out pizza. Layer cakes or bowls of chips. An elegant picnic basket or McDonald's from a paper sack. It's an invitation to belong.

Lounging. Relaxation. A Sabbath from work, from worry, from routine. A sweet deviation from the hectic pace of week-days and Saturdays full of chores.

Sunday dinners and lazy Sunday afternoons reminiscent of post-Thanksgiving meal bliss. Sitting around with dessert, languidly chatting, catnapping in a wide-armed chair, curling up with a book.

Finding out whose lap I could sit on to glean "grown-ups only" stories. Even as a grown woman, I would sometimes find my way to my father's lap, listening to his stories and seeking his advice. Indignant that I had usurped her place, Eden once told me to "Get off of Boppa's lap, Mama, you're taking up the whole family!" She too learned to cherish time-honored traditions like lapsitting, cuddling and Sunday dinners.

Sunday dinners are the practice of fellowship. The divine development of traditions.

There's a popular Martina McBride song that croons "love's the only house big enough for all the pain in the world." That love is found in our Father's House. One day the gates will be opened to a table set for the eternal feast. In will come the poor, the lame, the shamed, the broken and the broken-hearted at His invitation. There will only be one common denominator (for all of us are unworthy) and that will be our boundless love for the King, His Son and His measureless, matchless grace.

I'll never forget the sermon in which my father talked about forks and what they had to do with heaven. "Picture a holiday meal with family and friends all gathered around a picture-perfect table, fit for the cover of a magazine. An unbelievable amount of delectable food has been consumed. You've had seconds, and even sampled portions of thirds. You are stuffed. Simply too stuffed to even consider taking another bite.

The hostess gets up from the table and begins to clear away the dishes. The guests surreptitiously unfasten the top button of their pants. They smile, lean back in their chairs and groan in miserable satisfaction. 'I couldn't hold another morsel!' they announce.

And then the hostess makes her announcement. It's not unexpected, but it brings anticipation back to the table nonetheless. "Hang on to your forks, the best is yet to come!"

"Hang on to your forks!" urges the book of Revelation. "The best is yet to come!" promises Paul in I Thessalonians 4:13-18. "And so we will be with the Lord forever. Therefore encourage each other with these words."

Are you tired? Are you discouraged? Can't find your way out of the darkness? Didn't like the main course? Not fond of the people you were seated with? Just wait.

Sunday dinner. Eternal Feast. Taste of Home. Taste of Forever.

For a long time I carried around the plastic fork my father gave me as a reminder of my promised future. "I know the plans I have for you," says the Lord. "Plans to give you hope and a future." (Jeremiah 29:11) Eventually two of the tines broke off and it was worse for the wear.

But I haven't forget the message, and I want to remind heartsick, footsore people of that age-old promise: "Hang on to your forks, the best is yet to come!"

Chapter 16

## Old Memories, Young Hopes

*"We shape our dwellings, and after-*
*wards our dwellings shape us."*
— Winston Churchill

Her name was Linda, she was in the seventh grade of the first class I ever taught, and she smelled worse than rotten cantaloupe left on a roadside curb for three days. Breathtaking would have been the kindest word I could have said about her.

Strands of unkempt hair hung in greasy ropes, often hiding her eyes. Her teeth were crooked and discolored. Her clothes were don'ts, even for garage sales. She was a mediocre student on her best days, and for some reason, she adored me.

Each morning she stood by my classroom door awaiting my arrival. She also wanted to finger a pin, earrings, a necklace, a blouse, whatever I happened to have on that struck her fancy. "You sure do dress nice," was her refrain.

None of the kids at my small rural school liked her. Even if they had gotten past her clumsiness and painful shyness, the smell would have gotten to the best of them. A month into the school year, the situation reached crisis proportions.

I heard the rumors drifting in after lunch, and on the playground. "Someone tied a deodorant bottle to Linda's locker. You'd think she'd get the hint!" "That's nothing. Day before yesterday, we all put a punch of those potpourri stick-ups all over her locker door." "I think I'm gonna make a sign that says, 'You stink'!"

I called a meeting of my students and begged them to show pity, if not mercy. "Leave her alone, guys. How would you like it if someone treated you that way?"

Then one student pinned me to the wall. "She does smell pretty bad. Even you gotta admit that."

And there he had me. In the beginning stages of my first pregnancy, it was all I could do to keep breakfast down when she approached my desk for help.

So I did the only other thing I could think of. I went to Linda herself. She stood in front of my desk and sobbed. "They all hate me. They said I smell bad!" She reached out her arms to me and I hugged her gingerly, plotting to burn my clothes later. "Do you think I smell bad?"

I was caught. "Linda, we all smell bad if we don't take a bath or shower every day. i would smell bad too, if I didn't take a bath and use deodorant. Everybody sweats and especially in this heat!" (Our school was not air-conditioned.) "Do you know it's important to take a bath every day?" I ventured.

After we talked awhile longer she revealed that the water had been shut off often at her house for the past few months. Not only could she not shower, her clothing wasn't washed very often either. Arrangements were made for her to shower at the school locker rooms and to use the athletic department's washer and drier.

The first day she came to class in clean blue jeans with clean hair was a banner day for all of us. Another girl in class gave her a barrette and showed her how to pull her hair back from her face. And when Linda smiled, it was a different kind of breathtaking.

I moved after that year and never got to see Linda again.

But I often wonder if she remembers the hope in the gift of a barrette.

A few weeks ago I wrote notes home to the parents of a few of my high school students. I had made a resolution that I would not contact parents only with bad news, and these notes were part of it.

I called Jack* up to my desk and handed him a folded note. "Jack, do me a favor and make sure your parents get this tonight," I said poker faced.

He slouched away, head down and muttering. "Jack," I called, "You can read it if you want to."

He sat down at his desk and unfolded the paper and I went back to the piles of work on my desk.

Abruptly, Jake stood up and announced loudly, "Hey! This is a positive note! Did you really mean this? You like me? I'm improving?! Wow! I've never gotten a good note before in my whole life!"

Jack is a freshman.

I don't know the rest of the story, school's only been in session for three months. But he's quit skipping my class, and some days, he even smiles.

I first saw it engraved on a cedar hope chest in a musty antique mall—**Old Memories, Young Hopes**. It's a tough balance to achieve. If we don't have a legacy to look back on, we suffer.

Lot's wife couldn't resist looking back and she crystallized into a pillar of salt. She forgot that there's a huge difference between learning from the past, treasuring memories and wallowing in what we've left behind, what will never be again.

If we are so entrenched in the past that we can't look forward, we suffer. I've wrestled with this balance a lot lately.

It's not that I don't have water at my house, because I do. And it's not exactly that my water tastes, well, *bad*, because it doesn't. It's just that it doesn't taste like I remember the water tasting at my parents' home in St. Louis. My childhood home. Since leaving, quenching my thirst has never seemed as satisfying.

If I close my eyes, I can still taste the water's welcome coolness after mowing the lawn. I can still remember the exact flavor of the water, gotten on tiptoe, straight from the tap, filched in secret, long after I was to have been in bed. And I miss it.

In the midst of heated battle with the Philistines, King David got to reminiscing about the well he drank from in childhood. He was thirsty and he longed from a drink from the well near the gate of Bethlehem (2 Sam. 23:13-17). Apparently the longing was so strong, he voiced it in front of his men.

Three of his mighty men, braved enemy lines and snuck in to draw water from that well. They (proudly, I imagine) presented to the King. And he did the unthinkable. He poured it out on the ground! "Far be it from me," said David, "To drink this when it was obtained at such cost."

The mighty men might have been angry. But I think David recognized the value of the sacrifice and the memory that gift of water invoked.

Sometimes a drink from the cool water of memory does more to foster hope than you could imagine.

I think of this on beautiful autumn days after school, when I go up in our wooden play fort with the girls and we sit there with good books and popcorn, potato chips or cookies. We talk, we giggle, we laugh, we swap stories and sometimes we have our devotions up there.

A few weeks ago, we were studying Psalm 139. I gave the girls a memory verse about God forming us and knowing us when we were still in our mother's body. Eden got it down perfectly. Four year old Emmy translated it, ". . . in your mother's room." Two year old Ellie runs around jubilantly yelling, "God my body!" She gets the point.

I want my children to cherish such memories, for I know that I will. They will grow up too fast and there will be things that I'll miss. I will miss drilling Eden on her spelling words and times tables, swinging with her and writing together on the porch swing during her sisters' naps. I will miss Emily grinning at me goofily at the table and saying, "Hey, mommy! Watch me eat a carrot without barfing!" I will miss sleepy, pajama clad Ellie crawling into our bed to 'nuggle on Saturday mornings.

I will be left with sweet memories, but also with the very bright hope for their futures. On one wall in my bedroom is a precious picture of a mother rocking a newborn in a cradle. Another small child looks on. The mother smiles wistfully, the child looks down in wonderment. My husband remembered that I loved it and presented it to me on my 33rd birthday. Beneath the picture is my favorite scripture: " 'For I know the plans I have for you,' says the Lord. 'Plans to give you hope and a future.' " (Jeremiah 29:11)

It's important to have a hopeful future. Just ask my sister who was so traumatized by growing up with a bossy, older sister, she wrote an essay about it her senior year of high school. She described a Saturday morning childhood ritual. Before my dad mowed the lawn, it was our job to scoop up the dog's waste from the yard.

Conveniently, this was the only time I ever allowed her to

have the lead role in any of our dramas. Magnimoniously I granted her the part of Cinderella, while I played the Wicked Stepmother. Translation? I got to hold the trash bag while she did the actual scooping!

Were it not for God, we would have nothing but old memories and we would be forever doomed to play the role of Cinderella with no hope of Prince Charming's rescue.

We drove through the Taco Bell drive through last week in separate cars, a consequence of schedules, not choice.

All three noisy, hungry, grumpy children happened to be in my car. I ordered and went to the second window to pay. Suddenly it occurred to me that I could do a small thing to shake things up, teach a lesson and make a memory.

"How much is the gentleman's order in the car behind me?" I asked the teenage cashier as she snapped her gum.

"$2.85. Why?"

"I'd like to cover that."

Her blank stare gave way to raised eyebrows.

"Uh, um, okay, I guess."

I handed over the money.

"Do you know him?" she asked.

I smiled mysteriously. By this time, all three girls were stupefied and blessedly quiet.

"Do me one more favor, would you? When he drives up, will you tell him I think he's cute?"Another giggling teen had joined the cashier, openly listening to our conversation. The cashier girls nodded. I winked at them, smiled and drove off.

Eden exhaled and exploded with laughter. "Mom! That lady thinks your'e crazy! You are crazy! Why'd you do that?" What a memory.

And the lesson. "I love your daddy, girls, and I just thought he could use a reminder."

When we met up later, my husband was beaming, my girls were giggling and another bond was in place, glued with the cement of memory, hope and commitment.

Perhaps the offering of a simple glass of water, a small gesture, could mean more than we've thought.

A few evenings ago, Emmy looked at the great orange beach ball that was the sun, sinking down into an ocean of pink clouds and azure sky. "Wow, mommy! God does really good stuff!"

Yes, Emmy, He does. And that is what makes each memory precious and each new day a page full of hope.

So go home tonight and sweep your mate into your arms. Hold the face of each little cherub between your hands and dream their dreams. Rejoice in the finding of a new friend, a relaxing evening, a job well done. Remember that no matter what your situation, Someone is in control and He loves you.

Drift off to sleep in His astounding peace. And I wish you the best memories and the freshest of hopes while you do.

Chapter 17

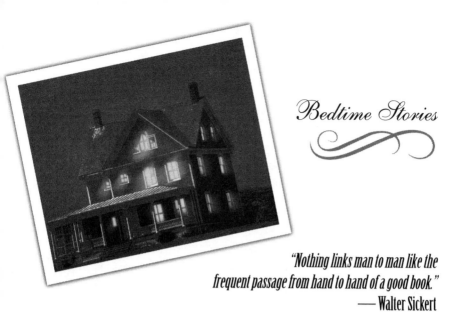

## Bedtime Stories

*"Nothing links man to man like the frequent passage from hand to hand of a good book."*
— Walter Sickert

*O*ne evening, just before bedtime, a little boy was reading a storybook in his room. As his father walked by, he noticed that his son was scowling, visibly upset. Poking his head around the door frame, he asked, "What's the matter, son?"

"I don't like this story daddy!" came the immediate response. "It's scary!"

Tenderly, the father patted the boy. "Better not read it any more then."

A few minutes later, when the father went back to check on his son, he found the lad happily reading the same book. A huge grin spread across his features.

Bewildered, the father said, "Son, I thought you didn't like that story. You said it was too scary."

"Oh, but daddy, I read ahead to the end of the story and now when the bad guy starts doing really mean stuff, I just shake my finger at him and say, 'Boy are you gonna get it! You're really gonna get it!'"

We too know the end of the story. Go ahead and read it. It's in Revelation. No law that says you must start at Genesis and read straight through (otherwise there'd be many a casualty in Leviticus, the graveyard of Bible study). One day time will be swallowed up. Pain and sorrow will be no more. The death march will give way to a victory parade, and Satan is really gonna get it! He will be bound for all time. I just love stories with happy endings.

When I was a child, the end of the day was possibly my favorite time. For at twilight, the lamps went on, cookies and milk were distributed, and we ate, spellbound by tales of heroes and heroines, brave pioneers, swashbuckling pirates, beautiful princesses and the princes who rescued them.

Stories of great Bible heroes: Moses. Joshua. Abraham. David. Matthew. James. John. Peter. The Apostle Paul. Floating basket beds, crumbling walls, a father of more than the stars, giant killers. Men who stopped *catching* fish to fish instead for men who needed the Bread of Life. Healers of the lame. A giggling tale of a man who was raised from the dead after tumbling from a high window, having fallen asleep during the sermon. A terrible tale of greed and lying to God and drop-ping dead after lying to Peter and the Holy Spirit. A God and a follower who walked on water. Survivors of ship wrecks. Earthquakes that opened prison doors. Stories of Jesus who loved children. A God who came to earth as a tiny babe and grew to be powerful, perfect and *real*. A heart stopping story of Someone who loved us enough to die for us. And then rose again.

As a child, bedtime meant the certainty of mother's lap and the tucking-in ritual performed by daddy who made the blankets into shapes around us. My sister, Angie, and I had contests to see who could hold still the longest without mess-ing up their shape. I always lost. And we would beg, "Just one more story? Please?" Then would come some of our most beloved stories. Stories from our past, detailing our legacy, our history, our heritage. Accounts of our escapades as toddlers, recountings of our parents' childhood adventures and the saga of their courtship. We never tired of hearing them, requesting our favorites over and over again.

My sister and I were thrilled by the stories and we learned from them too. Now that I am all grown-up with three precious daughters of my own, the bedtime story ritual is still a favorite of mine. I never tire of reading or concocting stories and then moving from room to room, kissing one sweet, sleepy face in a toddler bed; one precious face, that looks more like a young lady's every day, and finally tiptoeing in to the baby's nursery, and leaning over her crib to brush back escaping tendrils of hair and whisper, *"Mommy loves you."*

My girls love to hear the same old stories we loved as children. We tell them about the days we brought each of them home from the hospital. About how their daddy and I met (would you believe that a year before we actually met, he had heard me singing through my screen door while on patrol answering a call in my neighborhood and later recognized my voice?!) and about their grandparents.

I want them to have the legacy of it all. I put one special narrative into a story just for them. And then I mailed a copy to my parents, the ones who started it all and lived it out.

### *It is the bedtime story of A Love Like This. . . .*

It began in a small rural town. A friendship spawned in a one-room school house. They were sixth graders. She was rail thin, awkward and shy. She'd lived in town forever. He was tall, gangly and athletic. He was the new kid on the square. She thought he was handsome. He thought she had the prettiest hair he'd ever seen. But of course they weren't about to tell each other. So they engaged in all the typical behaviors of first-affection. Hair-pulling. Shin-kicking. Name-calling.

The town grew as did their friendship. She typed his high school papers. He helped out with frogs in science. She cheered his basketball prowess. He admired her acting ability on stage. She collected the class rings of other boys (three, to be exact) trying to get his attention. He pretended not to notice and told her spitefully that he wouldn't marry her if she was the last woman on earth.

My how things change. Their senior year they were cast in a play together. He played the husband. Her role was the wife. The last scene required a kiss. Later they both agreed it was intriguing.

After graduation they went away to college. Though he loved her, he dated many other girls, hesitating to tell of his love for her, wanting it to test its realness. Wanting it to last forever. She cried into her pillow, thinking he didn't care. She mistakenly took the engagement ring of another. He sat up and took notice. He asked her to call it off. She did.

A few months later, on a dimly lit dirt lane back in their small town, he took the hand of the girl whom he'd loved without acknowledgment since the sixth grade. Upon the fourth finger of her left hand, he placed a white gold band bearing a diamond solitaire. He'd decided to be a minister, devoting his life to God. He warned her about sacrifices she'd have to make. Of his time with her. Of material possessions. She smiled and said she didn't mind.

So he preached, ministered and served and wrote a column for the sports page of a different small town newspaper. They had a baby girl. Another town, another move and then they settled down. Another baby girl was born. Life was good, and the man had a dream of building a church for the God he felt had been so good to him. With four families and God in their midst, the work began.

The church grew along with the children. The four families grew into a church of over six hundred and three worship services. Those who needed to believe in God's goodness were drawn to Him in that church through the life of a man who lived every day like it was a gift.

But one day, the man was diagnosed with cancer. *It will take him swiftly and ultimately, it will cost him his life,* warned the doctor. But the doctor made such pronouncements without knowing the power of faith, or the prayers that would storm heaven's gates on his behalf. Still, the love of this man and his wife grew, bound up in a million different memories, cemented with the glue of commitment. For they did not take it lightly, this promise they'd made.

The little girls grew up watching this example as a pattern they dreamed of for their own someday loves. Before it seemed time, they left home, graduated from college and were married, blessing their parents with grandchildren.

Meanwhile, radiation and chemotherapy took its toll on the beloved father and husband. Preaching had to be curtailed for a time, and he did not always have the energy of his youth. Nevertheless the girls observed that he loved their mother through the changes that childbearing and middle age had wrought. That their mother loved their father right back, even when his chemotherapy made his hair fall out and then grow back, soft and downy as a baby duck's.

He cherished his bride of thirty some years, though her hair grew thin and tiny age spots appeared on her hands. She loved him when the cancer puffed up his face and then just as swiftly, changed and left him with the body of a scarecrow. The girls marveled and thought, *Not many people have a love like this.*

The miraculous gift of years passed, each day unwrapped with joyous anticipation, for they knew that *all* days given are presents. Then one day, all too soon, the doctor gathered the little family to tell them that miracles, perhaps, were coming to an end.

They watched their father tell the doctor how God had been good to him. He hated to say good-bye, but when the time came, whenever that might be, he would be ready to take the best seat in all the universe.

This is what love is. A father who learned of such love from his Father. A love that stands when all else has fallen. A love with a tenacious hold on each other; which keeps a vow made, even when that vow is painful. It endures. It is patient. It hopes. *It is a love like this.*

I watched this model of love lived out for thirty four years, six months, eleven days, eight hours and seventeen minutes. "'Til death do us part."

Daddy went Home at the age of fifty-six, exactly twelve hours after the birth of our third daughter, Baby Ellie. She was what he was waiting for and God was gracious enough to allow him to know of her arrival.

But there is another story, even better and more poignant than that. It is the story of a sacred romance. Of a God who loved us when we were unlovely. Who rescued us when we were undeserving. Who remained faithful when we were faithless. A God who was committed to us in the face of rejection. Who gave grace when we were not gracious. Whose love for us shouts from a cross and echoes from an empty tomb, calling us across the centuries.

The story of a Bridegroom who wooed His rebellious, cantankerous Bride and redeemed her again and again through its pages. Then He returned Home to prepare the honeymoon suite, and when He comes again, the joy will last forever. Amen. Let the honeymoon begin!

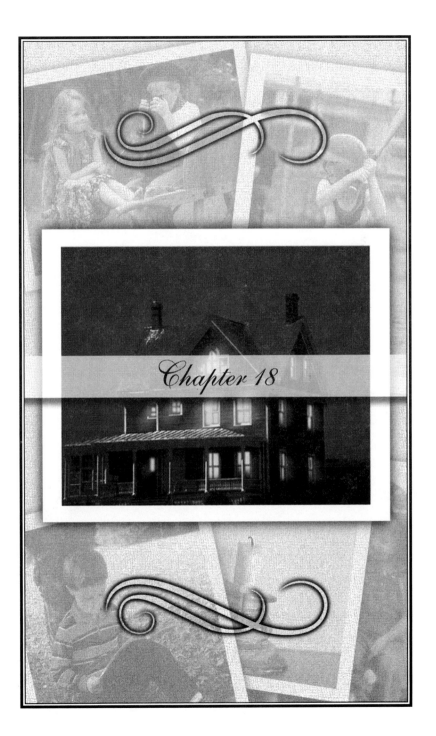

Chapter 18

# Welcome Home!

*"Home. A place where when you get there, you know your heart has been there all along."*
— Gloria Gaither

When I was a little girl, my mother began a tradition of making Welcome Home signs for daddy whenever he left to preach a revival or make an out-of-town business trip. The first offerings were meager attempts. Crayon tracings and rubbings of chubby baby hand prints.

As we grew, the signs became more elaborate. Markers, glitter, tempra paint. And with the advent of computer banner programs—look out!

My sister and I would wait eagerly, our noses pressed flat against the screen door glass, each trying to be the first to spot daddy's car before it pulled into our driveway. Fathers and homecomings are a magical combination.

Each night when Greg returns from work, my girls trip over me as if I were a mere ornament in the family room. Shrieking wildly, they yell, "Daddy's home! Daddy's home!" He is greeted with drool on one shoulder from the baby, a chubby-armed hug around the knees from the pre-schooler and frenetic jumping up and down from the 9-year-old.

I am sick with exhaustion just watching them. (For me to get such a reception I'd have to be kidnapped by aliens or at least have visited a foreign country.) Yet I remember greeting my daddy this same way.

And, I must confess, that I am not immune to the thrill of Greg's homecoming either. I too still feel the spark that smolders amidst the chaos and above the three small upturned heads. A gentle press of hands, a look passes between us that speaks volumes. Greg is home.

Whenever I am the one away from home, Greg will often call to tell me that the candles are lit in the window, not because he cares about such things, but because he knows I would have them on. And they will welcome me upon my return.

Homecomings are always special occasions. A flurry of expectation and anticipation always preceed them. We fly around adding special touches that show an arrival has been expected; a guest has been awaited with anxious anticipation; someone loved is returning home.

Recently it occurred to me that we should await the Lord's coming with just such enthusiasm. The early Saints did. They lived every day in breathless anticipation of His soon return! Paul's letters are full of the urgency of homecoming. Those first Christians looked for his return any day! Talk of the Second Coming was common, not just reserved for special days. In fact, they encouraged one another with that hope.

> "For the Lord himself will come down from heaven. . . .and so we will be with the Lord forever. Therefore, encourage each other with these words."

> (I Thessalonians 4:16-18)

We have a chance to pass on this love of homecomings to our children and our children's children. It's a race, writes the Apostle Paul. A race that no one will finish until Christ's return.

Our job is simple—pass the baton and then cheer like crazy. Do you ever feel like it's too late? You've dropped the baton? You're too tired to finish? You don't think you can do it on your own? Good news. You don't have to. You never did. Hebrews

Chapter eleven is a record of the greatest faith heroes ever. Some of them made mistakes. Adultery. Disobedience. Rebellion. Lying. Doozies. But the Hebrew writer is quick to point out: *"All these people were still living by faith when they died. They did not receive the things promised; they only saw them and welcomed them from a distance."*

That great cloud of witnesses is cheering us on, praying for someone else to finish the race, to make it safely Home.

And it won't be long. Look around you. On this earth are seeds of heaven. Precious glimpses of what we shall become. Just as when we look at our children we can see glimpses of the person they will be when they're grown.

In the way that our children fulfill our legacy and our dreams, we too are the fulfillment of God's desire. Our welcome Home will include crowns and an eternal banquet. We will be the King's guests of honor, forever, at the best party ever given!

Meanwhile, we enjoy the sweetness of home. Sweet busy-ness. Sweet rest. Sweet work. Sweet play.

When you write a sentence, sometimes there are things to be said that aren't the main point. Important things, just not the focus. So sometimes, we writers put such things in a set of parentheses. They signify a pause. To get to the best part of the sentence, though, you have to skip over the parentheses and read the end.

When life gets hard (as it invariably does) I take an index card out of my Bible. On the card I have drawn a simple set of parentheses. I look at them and remind myself that life here is just like that pause. The good stuff is still coming up.

Sigh. In the next room I can hear an alarm clock going off, incessantly buzzing, demanding my time; my presence at the next activity.

It reminds me of the box I made for my daddy when I was

in the fourth grade. I painted the cigar box my teacher handed out brown (a manly color, I thought) and shellacked it until it shone. I carefully selected a picture postcard of a cardinal perched on a flowering dogwood tree and pasted it on the middle of the box. On Father's Day I proudly presented it to my dad and told him it was for his special treasures.

Turns out he used it to store time pieces. . . .and therefore, pieces of time. I occasionally take them out of the box and turn each one over, feeling the history, the legacy, the essence of time I hold in my hands.

There is my grandfather's pocket watch, my great-grandfather's time piece, as he called it, and all the watches daddy ever owned in this life. Cheap plastic. Digital. With alarms and without. A gold-plated dress watch. A black plastic sports watch. Watches with worn-out bands. Watches with no bands.

All of them are still now, and it reminds me that time is fleeting. That time is precious. That in heaven time will be swallowed up. It will be no more.

No more waking to the shrill buzz of an alarm, dragging weary bodies out of bed for another day of toil.

No more yelling at the children, "Hurry up!"

No more fighting with our spouse about being late.

No more complaining about not having any time.

At last there will be no time.

Only an eternity to do whatever we love and to worship our First Love with no limits whatsoever!

Imagine taking as long as you want for a visit. A nap. Finishing a novel at one sitting. Uninterrupted. To gaze at the One who lovingly lingers over His return so that we can bring all of our friends Home with us. The One who gave us time and the One who will take away all the pressures that time entails.

There will be no boundaries. No limits. No weariness.

And as the beautiful chorus goes:
And oh, we will look on His face!
We will go to a much better place!
To live there forever. And He will welcome us Home.
"Welcome Home!" What warming words.

Think of it for a moment. If there is someone whose heart beats just a little faster when you pull into the driveway at night, someone whose nose is pressed against the window pane, waiting to wave wildly in greeting, someone whose footsteps quicken when they hear your key in the door, you are indeed blessed with welcome and with home.

Chapter 19

## The Lights of Home

*"Home is the definition of God."*
— Emily Dickinson

*O*h my goodness, Cindy, it looks like someone threw up Christmas all over your house!" my neighbor exclaimed. I took it as a compliment. At Christmas time our house becomes a wonderland of lights. We haunt the holiday sections of every store, admiring the festivity and searching for this year's addition to the lighted Christmas village pieces we collect. We visit the Holiday Barn tree farm and cut down our own tree, then we cart our treasures home. We drape lights on the tree and top it with a shining silver star. We entwine more lights with fragrant green garland and hang them from the rafters, wind them through banisters and tack them around the windows. The porch railings and posts also boast strings of lights, wrapped through boughs of pine and bright red bows. Luminaries line the drive. A large Victorian angel waves her candle-filled arms in the attic window and the porch light is changed to a holiday green. The glow of candles fills each room. There is not a corner of our home that doesn't speak of light and Christmas.

Perhaps I do go overboard a bit during this season that changes the world, for a few, fleeting, shining weeks into a preview of heaven. But when my girls help me unwrap each piece of the nativity set, explaining to me the birthday story of the Light of the World, I don't think so. Kneeling before the manger that housed a baby King, we are again in awe of such a Gift. Afterall it was the bright light of a special star which made the shepherds aware of the Christ of Christmas. The lights remind us of such things.

Jesse Barnes and Thomas Kincaide, the celebrated painters of light, certainly recognize the appeal and the connection between lights and home. Study their work and you'll find that what draws you to their scenes (other than the fact that these talented guys can paint like nobody's business!) is the light. Standing in front of a village street, an autumn barn, a church at Christmas or an ancient house bathed in the rich slant of a summer sunset, it is the light that makes you feel you are there. Causes you to wish yourself into the picture.

Our family has begun many a trip or vacation in the dark hours of pre-dawn and traveled well into the night. What keeps me awake, in fact beckons me, on my driving shifts, are the lights of the homes we pass. (Well, that, Funyons, M & M's and Diet Coke!) I love to spin stories to go with the lights.

> *Oh. I'll bet the tiny lamp in that window is a nursery lamp and a weary mother is up there with her lips pressed to the soft, downy head of her restless infant as she rocks and hums tuneless lullabies. . . In that house, a couple sits on the couch exhilarated with the heady wine of young love and chock full of wedding plans. . . The rays of the night light in that room fall on an old man in his eighties. He is tenderly holding the hand of his life's mate and as he places cool cloths on her forehead to soothe her fever. . .*

Fanciful, I know. But I can't seem to help myself. It's the call of the lights. The homes that seem happiest are the ones with the light.

Jesus said, *"When I am lifted up . . . (I) will draw all men to myself."* (John 12:32) Yes, Light crucified on a cross would do that.

When my precious daddy was diagnosed with cancer and it began to appear that it would not be long before he was called Home, we took a walk together. We spoke of many things. Memories. Silly ones. Serious ones. Goals. Dreams. He reaffirmed his great love for me and reminded me that he would always be proud of me, whether he were around to verbalize it or not.

I sobbed into his shoulder. I did not think I could bear a world without daddy. Together we picked out a star that I could look at and think of him while he was waiting for me to come Home. The top star of the big dipper. "Remember Whose you are," daddy said. "Miss you like crazy, but I'll see you again. Soon." That is perhaps something that we all need to be reminded of. When we gaze at the heavens with their sparkling lights and we long to be there, we can remember that we belong to the Maker of the stars, guarder of our footprints and architect of heaven. And it won't be long until we see the lights of glory, The Lights of Home.

And we have family there. All of us. No matter if perhaps your earthly family has failed you. Your Father is there, and you can't imagine the multitudes of brothers and sisters!

Anthony Brandt said, "Other things may change us, but we start and end with the family." How true.

It began in the garden of Eden. Adam. A lonely man. God gave him a woman, Eve, and this first family walked with God in the cool of the evening and lived together in paradise. Right up to the point where Eve decided to go shopping in the fruit section of the Tree of Knowledge of Good and Evil. With one crunchy bite of sweet, but forbidden fruit, they were cast out of Eden.

And God's redeeming work began.

It marched boldly through the pages of the Old Testament. Onto the ark with Noah and his family, the only ones who

remained faithful. Into Abraham's tent where He promised
the childless man that he would have more descendants than
there are stars; the Messiah would be among them. Watched
over the trouble that Jacob and Esau made over a mess of
pottage. Plummeted into the bottom of a well with Joseph
and delivered him to great heights.

Redemption wafted through the sands with Moses and
the Israelites as they marched from the Red Sea into a land
flowing with milk and honey (even though it took them forty
years)! It strengthened the hand of the shepherd, giant killer,
musician, friend and king, David. It graced Solomon's temple;
comforted Isaiah's people.

Then God's plan surprised everyone by tiptoeing into the
New Testament. For the Savior appeared, not in a blaze of
glory like the oppressed and weary Jews had hoped, but
clothed in infant garments. Swaddling clothes that were
traded for thread-bare tunics, work-worn sandals, a crown of
thorns and then, amazingly, empty blood-stained grave
cloths.

He conquered the fear of death for all time. He went to be
with His Father. And again, He turned the world on its ear, for
He left us to finish His mission: seeking the lost and leading
them Home. To a family of believers.

Luke 15 recounts three stories about lost things, including
the beloved story of the prodigal son. You remember. A
certain man had two sons, and the younger of them said to
his father, "Drop dead! I want my share of the inheritance
money and I want it now!" (Loose translation, but remember
that a will is not supposed to be in effect until the party dies.)

Then he took off. To a "distant country," scripture tells us.
At this point in the story, I like to switch to the King James
Version. Once there, "He wasted his substance with riotous
living." He lived it up. He had the latest togas. The best quality

sandals. The finest wines and gourmet foods. When the money ran out, apparently so did his friends. *"And he began to be in need."* (v. 14b) No kidding.

So he got himself a job, working for a foreigner. Feeding pigs. This may have been the boy's first job ever. Afterall, he came from a wealthy family. And what a job it was. Day after day he slopped the hogs. Ever done that? Me neither. Not personally, but I've seen someone else do it . . . and well, no thanks.

But to this guy, that pig food began looking pretty good. One day while he was slumped against the wood pile in the corner of the pen, a thought came to him: *The hired men in my father's house eat better than I do!* Scripture says, "He came to his senses." (v. 17) He experienced what Gordon MacDonald calls "a pigpen moment." I can practically see him smacking his forehead and saying, "Duh!"

He jumps up and paces back and forth in the pig pen rehearsing the speech he'll give to his father, the way we all rehearse things of great importance to us. *Dad, I really messed up. I sinned big enough to hurt you and all of heaven. I know I'm not even worthy to be called your son anymore, but that's OK. I'll be one of your servants. I just want to come home!*

In jubilation he leaps over the fence and begins the long journey back.

Meanwhile the father of this same son has been waiting for his prodigal to return. He loves and misses him so. Not a day goes by that he isn't out on the porch after dinner, craning his neck and straining his eyes, hoping to see his beloved son walking up the driveway toward home. He's gotten a bit older, a bit more gray, a touch sadder with every passing month. Still, he watches. He cannot bear the thought that his son might never return.

## The Lights of Home

One evening as the father sits in his familiar rocker on the porch reading the Jerusalem Gazette, he thinks he sees a blur just on the horizon over by the pasture where the cows are grazing. Nah, he shakes his head. *Got to go get these eyes checked.* He scans the headlines. Stock prices are down. The Pharisees are up in arms over some prophet from Nazareth. There's a sale on fruit at the market this weekend. He sighs. *Nothing new.* Lowering the paper to his lap, he buries his head in his hands. When he looks up, he's certain that there's a figure coming up the lane. Looks familiar too. The father stands up. Stretches. Cups his hand over his eyes to cut the glare of the sun. *Son? That's my son!* The father leaps down the steps and takes the dirt lane at a run.

The father throws his arms around his son and kisses him. "Dad," the son begins, I've really messed up. I've sinned against you and all of hea—"The father isn't even listening. He's too busy planning the party! "Look!" he beseeches anyone within hearing distance. "You remember my son, don't you? Well, he's come home!"

Arm in arm the two walk the rest of the way to the house together. Every light is on in a blaze of welcome.

There's something infinitely appealing about the lights of home. Whenever we arrive home after dark, the warm glow of the family room lamp and the smaller twinkling rays of candles beckon us to enter. If we've been gone any length of time at all, I feel my heart quicken. I can't wait to go inside! I turn around and look at my girls encased in car seats and seat belts. "Girls! We're home!" My husband smiles at me.

It won't be long now until I'm home. God's Word assures me of that. I can't wait to meet Him. And I know He understands that I am beside myself at the thought of seeing my daddy again. No, it won't be long. I'll fling open the gates of heaven and run up the driveway yelling, "Daddy! I'm home!"

one more time, the way I used to do here on earth. I have no doubt that he will run to meet me and hold me in sweet embrace. Then he will take my hand in his and lead me to bow before the throne of my Father.

When our family first moved out to the country and no artificial city light competed with the brilliance of the heavenlies, we often lingered outside to look at the stars. We took walks under them and tried to drive through them. On one such evening drive, the topic turned to my daddy (the girls' Boppa) and how much we missed him. But we cheered ourselves with the thought that Boppa was in heaven with Jesus and all of us would join him there someday. As we pulled into the driveway and the beckoning lights of home, Emmy, not quite three, pointed to the sky. With awe and wonder in her voice, she breathed, "Oh! Look mama and daddy, we can see heaven from our house!"

The Lights of Home. May it always be so.

Cindy loves to hear from
her readers.
Please contact her c/o
Covenant Publishing
Author Relations
P.O. Box 390
Webb City, MO 64870
or at
lightsof home@yahoo.com

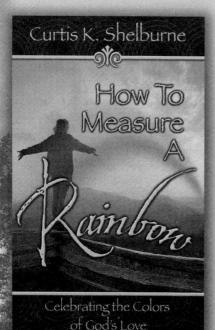

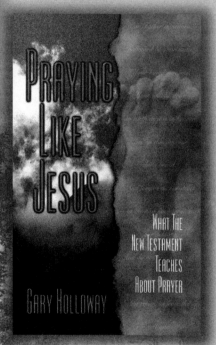